Barnsley
and Beyond

Barnsley
and Beyond

Mel Dyke

Wharncliffe Books

First published in 2007 by
Wharncliffe Books
an imprint of
Pen & Sword Books Limited
47 Church Street
Barnsley
South Yorkshire
S70 2AS

ISBN 978 1 84563 041 6

A CIP catalogue record for this book is
available from the British Library

Typeset in Sabon & Gill-Sans by
Phoenix Typesetting, Auldgirth, Dumfriesshire

Printed and bound in England by
Biddles Ltd, King's Lynn

Pen & Sword Books Ltd incorporates the Imprints of Pen & Sword Aviation,
Pen & Sword Maritime, Pen & Sword Military, Wharncliffe Local History,
Pen & Sword Select, Pen & Sword Military Classics and Leo Cooper.

For a complete list of Pen & Sword titles please contact
PEN & SWORD BOOKS LIMITED
47 Church Street, Barnsley, South Yorkshire, S70 2AS, England
E-mail: enquiries@pen-and-sword.co.uk
Website: www.pen-and-sword.co.uk

Contents

Foreword   vii

Special Acknowledgements   viii

Introduction   x

1   Sir David Attenborough • Sam Clegg •   1
Sir Michael Sadler • Sir Alec Clegg

2   Ian McMillan   21

3   Brian Turner   28

4   Pearl Fawcett   39

5   Stephen Smith • Charlie Williams   44

6   Graham Ibbeson   53

7   Patrick Cryne   64

8   Hudson Taylor   76

9   Jane McDonald   80

11   Joann Fletcher • David Moody   84

12   Derek Robinson   101

13   Tracy Wilkinson   118

14   Stephen Moody   126

15   Kate Kelly   138

16   Susan Johnson   152

17   Simon Hirst   158

18   Fiona Wood   168

Final Acknowledgements   192

Foreword

Our lovely audiences, readers and viewers are people who want real talent, real entertainment, real ideas, and they will find them in this book. This magical lady is a wizard of words who transports you to her wonderful world of sparkling imagery spiced with emotion, and exotically flavoured with Barnsley common sense.

She is not a poseur – but she does not disdain the occasional strut. Thank goodness!

Love and Happiness from Ken Dodd

Alex Durasow – AD Photography

Alex Durasow – AD Photography

Special Acknowledgements

The people in this book gave their time and trust by sharing parts of their lives with me, for which I am immensely grateful. Without their interest and help I would have had no stories to tell.

I am indebted to a great number of other people for all kinds of contributions, and their support is also gratefully acknowledged at the end of this book. There are others however, without whose extraordinary support the book would never have been completed:

Brian Elliott's own books on the history of the region and mining in particular need neither introduction nor recommendation, their quality speaks for them. As an editor he is tireless in his support and encouragement. As a friend he is generous and reliable in his judgement.

John Britton, with expertise and patience, ensured that there would be photographs in this book with contributions also from Dean Macfarlane and Aileen Cook.

James Britton repeatedly showed me the basic skills of using a computer without a hint of exasperation.

Elizabeth Ellis skilfully and patiently ordered my chaos into clerical and technological sanity.

Kevin Robinson spotted every slip along the way and humorously pointed them all out to me.

Charles Hewitt and his team at Pen and Sword were, as ever, most helpful and incredibly tolerant of my maverick ways.

My sincere thanks are due to Raleys for their support and sponsorship of the arts in Barnsley – including the launch of this book and *All for Barnsley*.

Amy Totenberg who, in inviting me to speak to her law students at Emory University, Atlanta, about my personal experience of the English education system, caused me to reflect more closely on how it did or did not work. Her wisdom opened windows in my mind and doors to teach me more.

Midge and John Sweet shared music and their historic home, complete with a thousand Inman Park tourists during my stay in Georgia, teaching me what civil rights are, and are not, in the USA today; and that learning, like history, is a cycle as beautiful as the Atlanta cyclorama.

Nina Totenberg warmly welcomed me to her home in a plum blossom Spring, and introduced me to a network as big as National Public Radio and politics in Washington.

Mary Valentine's Hollywood hospitality introduced me to the

Californian coast with sharp insight, tireless driving and a sense of humour that ensured we survived a night in the worst hotel in Palm Springs.

Fiona Wood showed me some of the west coast of Australia and gave me time she really didn't have as Australian of the Year; and threw in free medical advice!

My daughter Stephanie Watson raised my performance through her genuine interest, encouragement and constructive criticism.

My son Tim Dyke counselled me wisely, and gave me the comfort of reassurance in difficult days.

And, all proud to have Yorkshire in their blood, my grandchildren George Dyke, Mimi Watson, Charlie Dyke, India Watson and Benny Watson make my life fun, knowing exactly who they are and where they are from.

In *All for Barnsley*, Sir Thomas Elmhirst was described as Air Vice Marshal, for which I apologise. He was, and his family rightly remain, very proud of the fact that his rank was in fact, Air Marshal.

Introduction

He didn't have much time for teachers, George Bernard Shaw, with his 'Those who can, do; those who can't, teach!' Only someone who had never tried teaching could come up with that one. It started me out looking at the effects of education policy and practice and especially the place of the arts in the old West Riding of Yorkshire in the second half of the twentieth century. Trying to widen the perspective, to look further afield than Barnsley, I finished up going round the world. Again and again some coincidence would link me back. On the way I think that the world went pear shaped; not from global warming, but from arts cooling in educational policy in this country.

It's a fact; the dark satanic north no longer exists. The hills of the north are still here obviously, with many of the buildings that started out as textile mills, with some new style owners, and new style purpose. In 1983 for example, the entrepreneurial vision of Sir Ernest Hall and his son Jeremy created a new northern hub for arts, business, design and education from a vast derelict carpet mill in Halifax – Dean Clough. It was based on their belief that 'people crave to be successful and live in a beautiful world; and that civilisation depends on their achieving that ambition which requires the restoration of the creative arts at the heart of our society.' Jonathan Silver, literally following in the footsteps of Titus Salt, took Salt's mighty stone flagged mill buildings in Saltaire and with a lot of insight, a bit of a gamble and a little help from his friend David Hockney, created a different commerce and arts world at the old Salts Mill complex in 1987. Hockney was a magnet drawing new crowds to modern art in an old setting. It was a new kind of revolution, so subtle that it went largely unnoticed in the political heat of the decade, but heralded an awareness that was both commercial and stylish, and brought with it new interest in the resurgence of the arts.

Through local, national and international policies, ongoing regeneration replaces the out-dated mined and milled towns. Forty years worth of infra-structure of motorways, with increasingly loud rumours that the rail network will again function efficiently are bringing back to the north tribes who had long ago moved on. Favourable house and land prices, along with the replacement of steel, coal, docks, shipbuilding and fishing by call-centred commerce, light industry, technology and high class stores. There's a new allure and even a grudging acceptance that the pre-Norman sharp vowels equate with straight talking, and a work ethic that is the traditional norm. The sense of humour, unusual but infectious, has a rareness of pretension and comes with an ability to take people for what they are. And maybe the three ancient Ridings of Yorkshire represent some old English values, with an ancient tongue and a bit of cheek allowing the one to be placed more firmly in the other.

Being at the leading edge is not new to this renamed part of Yorkshire which was for centuries the industrial heart of wool, linen, coal, steel, wire drawing, and glass blowing. In the second half of the 20th century educational development flourished in the West Riding sustaining the reputation of a system which was a role model for other nations to adopt and adapt. At other times however it has systematically failed the very children for whom it was introduced. Change for the sake of change has quagmired vocation, good will and best intentions, just as politics, hidden agendas and controversy have dogged progress. At its worst, the education process in the West Riding of Yorkshire was a turgid veneer which stultified ambition and learning; at its best it was brilliantly unbeatable and inspirational.

That was due in no small way to the vision and efforts of a number of gifted people who despite being advantaged themselves, recognised and then opposed the imposition of disadvantage on others. Others, without such advantages, simply punched above their weight, persevered longer, worked harder, got lucky or took chances to find success. Today's 'celebrity culture' seems to limit aspiration, by encouraging imitation of those who are only famous; notable for being not able, and with little to celebrate. So here is a range of people whose efforts and results offer motivation and even inspiration to others. Linked in some way to the old textile or mining communities, they all have achieved success in some way. In my meetings with them and their families, education was invariably an issue. For some it was the quality of it which inspired them. Others, resenting the lack of quality, became more determined to succeed in their own ways with some interesting results. If it was not formal education which fired them up I was keen to know what it was.

Starting two hundred years ago with the Parliamentary debate which followed a Bill presented by Samuel Whitbread. It proposed that two years of free education be provided for pauper children to be taught the basic skills of reading and writing. It was opposed by Mr Davies Giddy MP for Hull who said:

However specious in theory the project might be of giving education to the labouring classes of the poor, it would, in effect be found to be prejudicial to the morals and happiness; it would teach them to despise their lot in life, instead of making them good servants in agriculture and other laborious employments to which their rank in society has destined them.

Instead of teaching them subordination it would render them factious and refractory, as was evident in the manufacturing counties.

It would enable them to read seditious pamphlets, vicious books and publications against Christianity; and it would render them insolent to their superiors; and in a few years, the result would be that the legislature would find it necessary to direct the strong arm of power towards them and to furnish the executive magistrates with more vigorous powers than are now in force.

Besides, if this Bill were to pass into law, it would go to burthen the country with a most enormous and incalculable expense, and to load the industrious orders with still heavier imposts.

(Hansard, House of Commons, 13 July 1807*)*

The noes had it and the motion was lost. With it went decades of educational opportunity and discarded potential.

Thank goodness no cynic would think today that the price of a child's education out-weighed its value. Would they?

Barnsley
and Beyond

Sir Alec Clegg
Sir David Attenborough
Sam Clegg
Sir Michael Sadler

David Attenborough is one of the most readily recognised names and faces on this planet, with a history of personal achievement that has earned him universal trust and respect. But what on earth, you may well ask, with the entire planet at his disposal, does he have to do with the old West Riding of Yorkshire? The link is tenuous I grant you, and untested, but in 1851 there was a George Attenborough living in Rockley Old Hall. By 1861 he had moved to live in nearby Worsbrough Hall, in the beautiful wooded valley that lies to the south of Barnsley and is part of the Yorkshire, Derbyshire and Nottingham coalfield. If David Attenborough's pedigree did not start in the coal bearing hills of the North, his educational roots certainly did. One of the first things he told me when I was fortunate enough to meet him, is how immensely proud of his maternal grandfather, Samuel Clegg, he is, and rightly so I find.

It was 1880 when free education was introduced in this country for all children between the ages of five and ten years, and in 1899 the school leaving age was raised to twelve years. The Education Act of 1902 replaced the old school boards, by creating local education authorities which were to be responsible for building and maintaining schools. It was potentially a time of new opportunities, expansion and change. Such change was envisaged, monitored and facilitated by government advisers of the day, including one of the most respected men in education, Michael Sadler. An outstanding educational pioneer, known as 'the patron of the arts in education', Sadler's own credentials were internationally indisputable. As a Trinity student at Oxford he learnt most from John Ruskin, and reviewed his hero's lectures as dealing as much with the economic and spiritual problems of English national life as they did Art. 'Let us reform our schools and we shall find little reform needed in our prisons . . .' became Sadler's mission. Despite a plethora of other offers of work, Sadler returned to Oxford and amongst his many

achievements there produced a syllabus for a series of lectures on 'how to better the conditions of the working classes past, present and future.'

It might be argued that Sadler was the architect of the bridge between elementary education and the universities. Certainly in 1893, by approaching the Hebdomadal Council, he was instrumental in setting up the first conference ever held to discuss how to extend secondary education in the UK. Held at Oxford University, it brought together public schools, school boards, universities, charity commissioners and, significantly, teachers' unions. He was an active leading member of the Royal Commission set up as a result of it. Interestingly, eighty years or so later another Oxford man would further a similar initiative. Derek Robinson, fellow of Magdalen College, was instrumental in ensuring improved access for working class children from state schools who ventured to apply to Oxford colleges. Visiting Darton High School in the 1970s, he met with the then headteacher and educational firebrand, Horace Crowther. Together the two ensured that a new generation of state school children was subsequently encouraged to apply for places at Oxford and other universities they had hitherto believed to be beyond their reach. The plan was cemented in the school's Individual Needs Unit, the first to be set up in the area; with a 'Clegg-trained' Head of the unit, whose philosophy was that gifted and talented children were as entitled to 'special needs' provision as the less able. The 1944 Education Act had referred to children of abnormal ability but funding had rarely followed beyond provision for those termed 'subnormal'.

Sadler's educational policy advice to the British government, based on his experiences in a wide range of foreign countries, led to his acceptance as pioneer and expert in the field of comparative education on an international basis. So it might have seemed a relatively routine task for him to report on secondary educational needs to nine local education authorities, including one for Derbyshire. It was however in preparing that report that Sadler found practical brilliance to match his own ideal. He came across a young art teacher who impressed him so greatly that his report said the man was 'a high voltage cable, electrifying and vivifying the entire community'.

The community was Long Eaton in Derbyshire and the young teacher, Sam Clegg, was then employed at Long Eaton Pupil Teachers' Centre. That report from Sadler in 1906 was accepted by Derbyshire County Council and led in 1910 to the creation of a new kind of higher Elementary School and Pupil Teacher's Centre, with Clegg as its first headteacher. Throughout their lives, Sadler and Clegg shared the value of teaching the requisite skills for a life of work. Equally they believed that this was best achieved through the development of pupils' understanding, of appreciation and of course, the application of the arts. In 1911, during a career of outstanding successes, before returning to Oxford to become Master of University College in 1923, Sadler was Vice Chancellor of the University of Leeds; the ironic significance of which later becomes clear.

This Sadler was of the same family as another Sir Michael Sadler whose work in the abolition of slavery movement is less well known than the East Riding's Hull born legend, William Wilberforce. Rare amongst their peers they shared the view that, ' . . . no man has the right to be idle' and included themselves in that philosophy. With its geographic proximity to Nottingham, the staple industry opportunity in Long Eaton, other than mining, was lace-making, which created a demand for workers who were 'skilled with eye and hand'. Clegg saw the potential in a system which provided a source for employers to have a trained a work force, offer a means of earning of living for workers, and lent itself exquisitely to the philosophy of using the beauty of the arts as a stimulant for relevant learning. Fortunately the like-minded County Surveyor for Derbyshire, GW Widdows, shared the vision and in total contrast to the traditionally austere and daunting Victorian school buildings designed a school which was light, airy and modern. Perhaps its most innovative feature was a centrally located, spacious, iron and glass art studio, where Sam Clegg would teach children and train teachers for the rest of his life.

In addition to the new bright and light building came an equally dramatic change in the style of teaching. Instead of receiving ex cathedra a piece of information, children from the age of twelve were invited to consider the reasons for the conclusion which might be drawn, and were actually expected to say if the stages in the argument were unclear. As important as this sharing of minds, was the start of a new routine; learning how to respect and share in caring for the environment. In keeping with the times, the regime was strict and the entire school was kept meticulously clean and orderly, with perfectly themed works of art in carefully matched frames, carefully selected and displayed on a wall in each room. No thumb print on a notice pinned up by one corner was allowed to mar the quality of any other aspect. Areas were reserved to provide space which was to be judiciously won by the quality of work produced by the children. Visiting artists showered their skills and enthusiasm on receptive eyes, hearts and minds, and children actively took part in producing work with them. Clegg himself supervised children working on three outstanding murals, one in each of three classrooms, a source of immense pride and pleasure in the school and community. Incredibly, after Clegg's death some years later, they were painted over in what was presumably an attempt to improve the décor. How fortunate Michelangelo was to have worked in Italy!

Art, Botany, History, Maths, foreign languages and English were linked across the curriculum towards an end product – lace making. Precision in drawing and painting, or appreciation of language through story-telling, was a routine aspect of lessons, as were visitors' inputs. One such visitor, a former Professor of Figure Painting at the University of Ghent, Mlle Rosa Vaerwyck recalled a childhood in Flanders, before poppies became its identity. With other Belgian refugees she brought a language, culture and experience that were readily absorbed into the school and the life of the community. The outcome of this was not racial tension, but distinctions throughout in the ensuing Oxford Local Examinations.

Along with English, Clegg's greatest passion was for his own specialism, the teaching of Art. Using field studies or simply pieces of fine lace, he taught how to transform growing plants into designs. Copying butterfly colouration led to painting, wood-block printing and embroidery. All planning was intricately designed to lead to greater understanding and pleasure in the development of requisite skills. A great favourite was the creation of books, produced by the children themselves, which entailed expertise in lettering, gilding and binding, and of course handwriting. Similar exposure to original, perfectly executed illuminated printing created a respect not just for beauty but also skill, and a desire to recreate it. Twenty years or more after leaving, former pupil Sir Harry Godwin FRS, Emeritus Professor of Botany, University of Cambridge vowed he could walk through the streets of the town and still identify the houses of others of Sam Clegg's former pupils 'by the appearance of their window hangings, furnishing and decoration'.

Clegg had a son Alec, a school friend of Godwin, and a daughter Mary, who married a former pupil teacher who joined the staff of the school in 1913. This equally fervent educator and great, if occasionally quirky character, Frederick Attenborough, was remembered with equal fondness by his pupils at Long Eaton not least for salvaging a potentially unfruitful RE lesson with the unforgettable call, 'Remember, the two most important things in life are Scripture – and football.' He was to become Principal of University College, Leicester in 1931, just a year after the sudden death of Mary's father, who had been working in his school only two days earlier. Attenborough became a red-brick revolutionist, choosing Leicester's one hundred and twenty undergraduates over Cambridge, which he had found 'intolerably back-biting and back-stabbing.' There being no government funding available this relatively tiny college was supported by philanthropists, and grew in both size and stature during his time in office.

It was Godwin's view that the breadth, imagination and incisiveness of Clegg's mind and ability as an educator could only be '. . . a natural swift eruption of genius for learning and the gift of perceiving how best to develop a love of learning and culture in young people.' Many years ago he identified the same genius in the young David Attenborough. This son of FL Attenborough, and grandson of Sam Clegg, was in 2006 voted the Most Trusted Person in the UK. So I can readily accept the very first thing Sir David Attenborough tells me when we meet, which is that amongst his many uncles, Sam Clegg's son Alec was always his favourite. 'He was perceptive, honest and completely straightforward, but also one of the best practical jokers I can remember. He once came to join us on holiday in Anglesey and spotting the whole family on the beach, instead of walking down to join them drove on un-noticed to the next bay. There he donned his trunks, waded in and swam back around the headland. The first we saw of our uncle that day was this figure walking out of the sea towards us. Since we thought he could do anything anyway, we naturally accepted the idea, and believed for years, that he had swum all the way across the Menai Straits to be with us.'

Sir Alec Clegg. *Lady Clegg's collection*

It seems that there was nothing that Alec Clegg could not turn into a game or a learning experience. 'However long the car journey when we were very small, my brothers Richard, John and I were never bored when he drove. He used very simple tricks to keep us involved, like increasing speed over bumps in the road, which he said were 'oo-ers' because of the effect they had on your stomach. We would measure the 'oooh factor' and compare it to the last one, or to predict the next one, but also try to work out if it was the speed or the steepness of the bump that caused it. Or he would spot and point out a church spire in the distance on his right, and a few miles later appear surprised, suggesting that the same spire must have hopped over the road as it was now on their left. There would be non-stop chatter until one of us worked it out. 'He had a terrific sense of humour too, told great jokes and was very good company. We just loved Jess his wife, a former primary teacher, and also a teacher of dance too; she was always, and still is so elegant and extremely beautiful.'

Hearing Sir David Attenborough describe his happy, fertile childhood, it is clear that disparity in children's early learning opportunities offends him just as it had Sadler, Samuel and then Alec Clegg. Having in earlier years regarded him as an expert presenter in biology, zoology, botany, geography and natural history, I now see just how brilliant a natural teacher he is. So good in fact that for all those years I had watched and read his work, I had failed to recognise that my interest and learning were the result of the ease and quality of his teaching. It flashes across my mind that the 'new approach' in our schools for the future, and our teacher training programmes, now put learning before teaching . . . 'There are no differences between education and entertainment,' he asserts, 'like all things that are worthwhile, the best comedy is educational, usually an insight into human characteristics. From Porridge to the wit of Shakespeare, it's so much better than throwing pies.'

'We were encouraged by our parents and grandparents, as well as by Alec, always to look beyond the surface and then to convey the notion of the unseen.' It is his boundless enthusiasm and palpable joy of doing that which has taken viewers and readers with him for over fifty years. Years of fascinating, enriching contributions of a range of quests to understand and to see more closely than we ever dreamed possible the lives of plants, birds and mammals – private or otherwise, on land, sea or air, and most recently in the undergrowth and cold blood. 'That's where technology has enabled us to go further, speeding up filming and allowing us to reveal the previously invisible,' he tells me. 'For me natural history isn't a subject, it's a series of adventure stories.' For his elder brother Richard the adventures were played out through film and theatre.

Alec Clegg's own route in to the profession and vocation of teaching began with a degree in Modern Languages at Clare College, Cambridge, followed by what he described as ' . . . perhaps the luckiest thing that ever happened to me.' He went to the London Day Training College and was a student of what was described as the most distinguished trio of educationalists of the day, including Cyril Burt. This induction and experience never left him and would in time become a dream of another kind.

From 1937 to 1945 he worked as an administrator in three local authorities and learnt something in each of them. As he was the first administrative assistant ever appointed in Birmingham, there was no lead to follow, so he took it upon himself to work in every section of the department including the schools. This was how he met a 'very pretty assistant mistress teaching at Paganel Road Infants' School' who was to become his wife, and the mother of his three sons. These personally fulfilling years contrasted sharply with the poverty he was witnessing following the years of the national depression. This was his grounding for understanding the problems and the potential of children from poor, disadvantaged or recidivist families in overcrowded, neglected and badly housed areas of the city.

Increasingly, as he became more aware of the effects of extreme deprivation and poverty, he stored positive aspects and examples of excellence, some forty years before Centres of Excellence were 'discovered'. He also worked with a Chairman of Education, Byng Kenrick, who epitomised for him what a person who opted for public service could and should be. 'He was utterly fearless, utterly dignified and utterly honest.' The young Clegg's mind, keen and receptive, storing this early but sound administrative perspective, then built it on to his own experience, observations and teaching practice. This was the basis of a modernised, gentler philosophy than his father's, and one that was to put the West Riding of Yorkshire at the forefront of the development of education in the second half of the twentieth century.

But before that was to happen his move to Cheshire in 1939 coincided with evacuation of children from Merseyside to that area, and the accompanying problems of integration. Clegg's personal view was that he did not have a positive experience in the placement, which he regarded as petty, bureaucratic and worse, and later said, 'I left it with a bad taste in my mouth.' He took it all in though as a deficit role model, and in 1942 left to become the first Deputy Education Officer for Worcestershire. His own account of the difference between the two posts was, 'In Cheshire I did a technician's job, in Worcestershire I began to realise what "professional" in the running of a great human service really meant.' Up to this point he had worked in two very different

Sir David
Attenborough.
The Author

8

systems, in each of which the aim was 'the efficiency of the machine.' Now in his third authority, for the next three years, the priority was 'the quality of the product' and he found himself part of an amazing and exciting team of visionary practitioners of excellence – and a new way forward.

In 1945 Alec Clegg arrived in the West Riding of Yorkshire, where he would spend the rest of his life. With him came colleagues from Worcestershire and elsewhere, cherry-picked from wherever best practice was known to be. Increasingly, the appointments grew and he formed, and would continue to expand, a team of remarkably able 'advisers' as they became known. They were, and remain, a rare breed. His greatest admiration was that, 'These folk could all "do it," they could teach as well as talk about it, and their expertise was recognised and welcomed by teachers.' Opposed to copycat systems, which appointed less able people but which had similar expectations, he warned that maybe one in ten had the 'power and gift' that would change teachers and schools.

In identifying people with qualities of 'élan and zest', and gathering them about him Alec Clegg was becoming a similar kind of high voltage conduit that his father was. Similarly, he took on board the benefits of beautiful surroundings, in which children would be motivated and the Arts, Music, Textiles, Drama, Movement and Dance would be used as vehicles to transport them. The days were numbered when forty military marchers or flitting fairies would collide on a crowded, cold, parquet-tiled hall accompanied by a pianist thumping out Percy Grainger's *Country Gardens*, whilst providing diversionary entertainment for grinning faces behind glass-windowed classroom doors. New, modern schools with gymnasia and custom-designed craft and practical areas sprang up to accommodate the growing population.

It was clear to Alec Clegg that the Education Act of 1944 alone would never be the universal education panacea that some still dreamed. There was much to be done in retraining and motivating staff rooted in old methods, and in spreading the best of philosophy and again, the practical application of it. By the end of the decade, with the foresight and unstinting support of the West Riding County Council and its Chairman, Alderman Walter Hyman, and by using the skills of his painstakingly garnered team, he was able to design and create a wide range of excellent training facilities in a collection of beautiful old buildings.

One of the largest grand houses in England, Wentworth Woodhouse, became a college of education for the training of women teachers of physical education, with a new emphasis on dance and the arts as well as retaining games and gymnastics. The family seat of the Lords Allendale, Bretton Hall, with its stunningly beautiful two hundred acres

9

of woodland and lakes, became a college of music, art and drama. Indelibly carved into the stonework of one of its buildings beneath his proudly inscribed name remain words from a Clegg childhood, kept in heart and head throughout his career:

> If thou of fortune art bereft
> and of thy earthly store have left two loaves,
> sell one and with the dole,
> buy hyacinths to feed the soul.

Grantley Hall became a centre for adult education; Woolley Hall was turned into Britain's first residential in-service college for the further education of teachers, and Ingleborough Hall, Netherside Hall and Nortonthorpe Hall became special schools. The National Camps Corporation buildings at Bewerley became a centre for outdoor pursuits and the former Wells House Hotel in Ilkley was adapted as a college of what was then known as housecraft. Bramley Grange provided training for teachers in further education. This high quality initial and continuing in-service training of teachers provided a springboard of opportunity for local adults as well as a national influx in response to the county's swiftly growing reputation for quality. In 1965 Alec Clegg was knighted for his contribution to education and elected President of the Association of Chief education Officers.

Recalling his own early successful experience, Clegg pursued the dream of a Day Training College for teachers in Yorkshire. Originally based in a secondary school building at Swinton, it was overwhelmed with applications from mature students, many failures themselves of previous educational folly. Within five years Lord Boyle, Her Majesty's Minister for Higher Education celebrated its re-opening in a custom designed building, a modern version of Long Eaton at Scawsby, in the heart of the coalfield. Its students were welcomed into schools across the West Riding, most of them remaining to stabilise teaching in the area after qualification, exactly as Alec Clegg had planned. It produced a wealth of teachers, of the arts but also of every subject across the curriculum at every age level from 4-18 years. New schools were provided to accommodate the swelling population of the area as the nation's demand for coal re-deployed thousands of mining families from the dwindling coalfields of Wales, Northumberland and Durham into the county.

For some of its alumni it was a stepping stone; English specialist Brian Glover stole the film in his debut as the sports teacher in real-life sports teacher Barry Hines' iconic 'Kes'. Roy Clarke, writer of the home-spun Holmfirth-set *Last of the Summer Wine* was another of its earlier

Brian Glover in his first teaching post with Head of English, George Hunter in the days when teachers had a break. *Picture by courtesy of Margaret Hunter.*

successes. Its legacy, quality and impact are still in evidence in the schools I visit today and to the second or third generation. I'd claim that despite the wonderful Three Tenors and a world cup anthem, no-one has done more to bring a love of opera to the widest of audiences than Lesley Garrett. The last person to lead a capacity crowd at Wembley for the final Cup Final she was as rapturously received at the equally historic Hollywood Bowl. Despite such international success she remains loyal to her roots on the banks of the River Don. Due in part to a 'no nonsense' approach to every kind of music, her incidental teaching of the subject ensures that it is fun as well as learning curvy. The daughter of two teachers, both former students in Clegg's training colleges, she deliberately encourages ambition in others recalling that her father's move from railway signalman to headteacher was what made her ask why a Yorkshire girl couldn't become an opera singer.

Those of us who trained and worked in West Riding schools in those provision-plus and paperwork-minus golden days remember still the nascent excitement of 'delivery day' from his West Riding museum service. Alec Clegg's administration added unprecedented access to a wonderful world of resources for schools through a county wide schools' museum service, providing for schools an impressive collection of original paintings and sculptures. It sparked harvests of optimism; stories, sculptures, collages, sketches, poems, displays of drawing and painting to line the walls and fill every corner of organised and quietly buzzing classrooms. The learning experiences spilled out into areas where Environmental and Rural Studies were taught as children grew vegetables and flowers and cared for livestock. No need then for celebrity chefs to invent awareness of food sources and healthy eating. The routine inclusion of cookery and housecraft in every school's curriculum ensured that however disadvantaged the background, children were able to become involved in preparing and sharing food in a way that was an enjoyable as well as empowering experience.

Anything and everything was a stimulant, from theatre and museum visits, field trips, experience of going down coal mines, visiting factories and remaining local mills or just walks in the surrounding woods, hills and valleys in changing seasons. First-hand visual, tactile and olfactory sense experience became as common in practice as auditory learning had been, as a result of these changes in the approach to in-service training and initial teacher training. Increasingly, classroom doors traditionally closed, were left open, or lessons would take place outside classrooms in the deliberate ferment Clegg and his team provoked as they challenged with their new ideas and methods. And with them came a sea change in staffroom debate. No longer was the war about who had more or less teaching time, the best or worst classes, the most cover periods for absent colleagues, the hottest or coldest classroom, the biggest allocation of capitation or the most marking or reports to fill in insisted. 'Walk and gawk won't work' the old guard insisted, 'Chalk and talk doesn't either,' the new enthusiasts would riposte.

The management line was clear; the responsibility should no longer

lie with the child to learn, but with the teacher to facilitate that learning. However, already there were worrying signs from the USA of teacher accountability being at risk of becoming a serious scapegoat. In Iowa a teacher had been sacked because the class was unable to manage the state's accountability tests satisfactorily. Clegg firmly held to the belief that social background was the key factor in a child's ability to learn.

Lesley Garrett. *The Author*

Children of professional, well-educated parents had a clear advantage over those whose parents had not completed their own education and had subsequently remained in unskilled jobs. It followed that results from the former groups would predictably be better than groups from the latter socio-economic groups. His concern was that blaming the teacher for an inability to produce the same results from groups of different abilities risked a new division of inequality. It would not only further damage the potential and morale of teachers, but also of lower ability children, possibly depriving them of the 'better teachers,' who might opt to teach in schools which would not risk them being seen as 'failing'. I shared this view then, and have a similar concern today, that the use of league tables continues to pose a similar risk from so-called parental choice and a clearly emergent 'sink school' status for some.

His concern was also strongly against examination systems, which he felt were equally largely divisive, and he favoured the course work system of the Certificate of Secondary Education. The potential dangers of that he could not have foreseen, and again the debate rages in the 21st century. An examination system which has become heavily weighted towards course work defies invigilation, and can provide an easier living for counterfeit essay writers peddling plagiarism on the internet, than teaching has ever offered to diligent and professional teachers.

Clegg warned that the Education Act of 1944 was misinterpreted and that '. . . if the only challenge we can offer the young is that of material prosperity we over-value the quick who can add to it and discard the slow who cannot.' He predicted the bitterness and discord in society that this would lead to, as 'the former will despise our values and the latter will resent our indifference – and we shall blame both for what is our failure.' To offset that risk he initiated a new series of highly regarded and successful courses offering in-service training and career prospects to experienced and proficient teachers, to enable the setting up of supportive and efficient Special Educational Departments in mainstream schools. This was, in my experience, one of his most effective actions, in a lifelong battle to redress the imbalance of provision for the disadvantaged. Late developers, long term absentees, the disaffected and children with physical and moderate learning disabilities flourished and achieved in the new warmer climate in which they found themselves.

Not all his ideas were successful, the debate rages still as to the effectiveness of keeping children in primary schools systems to the age of fourteen. He fought hard for what he truly believed in, but would make changes if presented with a chapter and verse argument, or practical evidence of what was or was not working at the chalk face. Some initiatives were tried and tested and eventually discontinued as less effective than had been envisaged, like open-planned classrooms or similarly laid out schools. Unless the teaching could be timetabled for quiet or interactive sessions across the entire school, noise from one area was often carried into another, disrupting both learning and teaching.

But he, like Michael Sadler and his own father before him, would never have changed his view on the singular importance of the arts in teaching. Bretton Hall became immensely successful as one of the best in training undergraduates in Performing Arts as well as teachers who would teach Music, Dance, Drama, Art and Design, English and Design Technology. It produced some quite outstanding names in those areas through both undergraduate and post graduate teacher training courses. In the late 1990s, following a series of intense HMI inspections, Bretton Hall College of Higher Education merged with the University of Leeds. Its arts courses were integrated into the university's own post graduate courses, in some cases winning high praise in the ensuing HMI inspections of Leeds. Michael Sadler, no doubt, would have seen that full circle, and approved.

The University of Leeds celebrates still its proud memory of, and association with that internationally revered former Vice Chancellor. Sadler, a man with an eye for great teaching talent, had also spotted and purchased early work by an unknown Russian artist, Kandinsky. Sadler's support led to the first showing in England of Kandisky's work I am grateful to be reliably informed by photographer Chris Sedgewick who, I suspect knows as much about Sadler's collections as anyone. These pieces are amongst the extensive collection of art including Ruskin, Millais, Gainsborough, Edward Lear and Turner which Michael Sadler bequeathed to Barnsley Cooper Art Gallery. I have to wonder what that 'patron saint of the Arts', the man who had been responsible for supporting Sam Clegg's philosophy and appointment in Long Eaton would have made of this century. Exactly one hundred years after Sadler first discovered Sam Clegg and set the ball rolling for their shared faith in the power of the arts in education; and either influenced or constrained by government policy, the same university took a decision to close down every last arts based teacher training course in the School of Secondary Education. Bread without hyacinths now it seems would be the diet for the future. 'Purely financial,' I am told when I query the need for it. Finance, finance, finance; is it then, Mr Blair?

We shall need more of the likes of Sedgewick when no more new teachers trained to the values and standards of Alec Clegg's vision for Bretton Hall, preserve the strength of the arts in the schools of the West Riding. No more students to carry the pollen of new development or tried and tested philosophy, with bright eyed enthusiasm and their love of music, drama, design, textiles and art into classrooms interacting with responsive teachers and children who want to learn. Pray God that does not mean there will also be no more of the likes of Sir Ken Robinson, John Godber, Richard O'Brien, David Rappaport, Kay Mellor, Beattie Edney, Mark Thomas, Colin Welland, and three out of four of The League of Gentlemen; not to mention Henry Moore, Barbara Hepworth, Elizabeth Frink, Graham Ibbeson and so on *ad infinitum*. And Peter Murray's wonderful Yorkshire Sculpture Park will live on without the close friendship and mutual co-operation of thirty years.

What does remain intact of what was Bretton Hall is the National Arts Education Archive Trust. These amazing and varied collections of papers, letters, artefacts, writings, paintings and drawings, including many by children, have been in the care of Trustees, including Lady Clegg, since Sir Alec's death in 1986 to the present day. For her they are living testaments to his dedication for what he called 'the end product of education' – the children, for whom encouragement and recognition were his banners.

It is inconceivable that such a legacy should be lost in political quagmire, and it isn't. Predictably, Alec and Jess Clegg's three sons all attended the local secondary school, went on to university and in one way or another, became involved in education.

With a Doctorate in Chemistry, the eldest, Andrew Clegg, began work as a science teacher in the West Riding, moved on to Taunton and finally to Botswana where he became involved in teacher training. Additional experience in Tanzania and Namibia led to his appointment as Physical Science Co-ordinator of a project to provide in-service training for Namibian science teachers. His work now includes involvement in the organisation of curriculum development in science in the Yemen, Qatar and most recently Nigeria.

John Clegg taught English in Germany before becoming a Principal Lecturer in English Language Teaching at Thames Valley University. Specialising in education through a second language, he has worked extensively with teachers in multilingual primary and secondary schools in the UK and in Africa. Now a respected freelance educator and teacher-trainer, he works primarily in Europe and Africa often in collaboration with the British Council. His publications in his specialist field and his contribution to the 'Challenges' handbook accompanying a BBC six-part TV series in 1979 remain relevant in today's global world. 'How do you fit in with other people's ways of living?' is the first prophetic question it asks. Both men, like their father and Michael Sadler, are Oxford graduates and both continue to contribute to the vision of development of teachers, and of education.

The youngest brother, Peter, is a Cambridge and Yale man, though with an Honorary Doctorate from Oxford Brookes, whose contributions impact on education in a different way. A Visiting Professor at the

University of Bath, he is actively involved in low energy architecture, research and environmental design. After re-designing the old Bothy Gallery at Bretton Hall in order to present a number of small individual display areas, he became architect in charge of the architectural development of the Yorkshire Sculpture Park at Bretton Hall. (The architect of education for the West Riding would have liked that one I'd wager.) Peter Clegg's other work includes a Science Park near Bristol, a new Performing Arts complex at Bath Spa University; and, most interestingly, a new Quad Arts and Media Centre in Derby – just down the road from his grandfather Sam Clegg's school in Long Eaton. Quality teaching and highlighting of the Arts and back full circle; and how Michael Sadler would have loved that.

Not one to suffer fools gladly, Alec Clegg could be a stern critic. He was however an equally astute judge of character who, recognising genuine ability would support, promote and delegate responsibility without hesitation. He could thus enable himself to make school visits on a weekly basis, using the experience as research and a sounding block for on the spot views and perspectives. Thirty and forty years on I meet people who will still quote the personal word of praise they had from him, others silently keep the stinging shrewdness of his observations to themselves. He had a fund of real stories of after-dinner circuit quality; anecdotes about people he met and things that actually happened. But, unlike some circuit performers, he unfailingly gave the credit to the real source if the stories were not his own, and took the flak if the story was against him personally.

The local dialect and accent used in the way children from the mining villages spoke fascinated him, to the point of publication. The satisfaction was in no small part due to the way his policies helped release that flow of creativity in 'the excitement of writing' from children. Taught well, they were inspired and produced incredibly original prose and poetry. Taught badly, they were bored to the point of inertia or avoidance. As a student observing a class of nine year olds listening to a story being read aloud I overheard a whispered conversation between two boys. 'Oh great; look it's snowing,' said one. 'I've seen it,' muttered the other, 'but dun't say owt, or she'll 'ave us writing about it.' And of course there were occasionally threats to the integrity of the system through the lack of professionalism of an individual here and there. On admiring the quality of displayed art work in a reception infant classroom on a visit early in my training I was given the following memorable advice. 'You sometimes have to add a bit yourself for it to be good enough to go on the wall, so if you do always use your left hand to do it, then it looks as if they've done it themselves . . .'

Alec Clegg knew well of this 'band wagon' risk and the danger of schools which were happy to call themselves progressive, whilst their children made no progress. 'Too much tissue paper filling outlines drawn by a teacher, writing which is artificially fancy, noisiness which comes from a lack of purpose, meaningless displays, groups working side by side on incompatible activities, and work of a low standard,' he shrewdly reported when he found it. He and his team were aware of individual teachers and worse still, Heads who ran schools which were 'like a wet playtime all day.' They oversaw 'inadequate record-keeping, poor organisation, failure to train children to prepare and clear away properly, could not distinguish between effort and achievement, did not know how to observe, ask the right questions or when not to intervene.' He exposed their hiding behind jargon and accused them of 'covering a multitude of trivial and unrewarding activities' by so-called 'projects'.

I think he must have been talking to Beverley, a nine year old pupil I met once in an educational priority area school. She had been 'doing her project' on frogs since the previous September and up to my visit around Easter the following year. Unmarked and possibly previously unseen, it ended with the most succinct and evaluative comment I think I have ever seen:

'While I have been doing this project I have got to know a lot about frogs. More than I wanted to know.'

There was a risk that with an area as immense as the West Riding, only the most important matters would get to the man himself. Not so. Letters from individual pupils, parents and teachers were all dealt with alongside those from international figures in the world of education and every Headteacher in the authority. Sir Alec Clegg rooted out what he called 'jiggery pokery' by running an open system which made information sharing a routine procedure, thus making his disappointment, dislike or displeasure known. Matters would then be rectified at the point where the problem had arisen. He condemned petty conspiracy, cliques, nepotism and what he termed 'wangling,' which was any attempt to try to get a particular person into a particular post or promotion.

Sitting as a member of a WRCC divisional executive education committee in the 1970s, I was present at just such an attempt to promote someone who was universally known to be both less qualified and committed than other candidates for headship of a department in a large local school. The candidate (son of a local politician) was personally well known to other members, though his performance and competence must not have been. By the narrowest of majorities, approval for his appointment went through along with a number of other appointments. It alone was returned to our next meeting stamped 'Not approved' and duly signed by A B Clegg himself.

As I watch Sir David Attenborough modestly accepting his award and acknowledging a genuine standing ovation at the 2006 ITA Awards ceremony in November 2006, in recognition of fifty years of an incomparable and positive contribution to broadcasting, it's clear again. It isn't enough just to have a family connection; that alone is unlikely to lead to any kind of real success, it is totally unacceptable to use that as a substitute for ability or talent. Luck may be a factor, but work and natural ability, nurtured within a caring environment of challenging motivation, are the ideal. When this is further enhanced by integrity, a boundless work ethic and an insatiable and lifelong desire to look, listen and learn we get Attenborough achievements. We then look on as after receiving his award, Sir David Attenborough courteously responds to a young man with a microphone in his hand. Referring to him throughout as 'Sir Attenborrow' the totally overwhelmed, or seriously underprepared, young man then briefly shares his own experiences of 'conservancies' in Namibia. I find myself asking: how on planet earth did this lad get this job? and I'm wondering if this is what they mean by the X Factor?

Clegg's empathic understanding of children from a world so far removed from his own, and that of his nephews, was quite remarkable. Like the Attenboroughs, he dedicated a lifetime to redressing imbalance by addressing the issues. He had a great love for the West Riding of

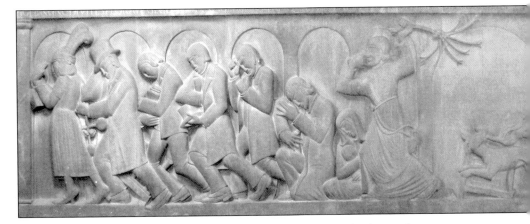

The base relief commissioned by Sir Michael Sadler which stands in a building of the University of Leeds, named after him. A modern version of Christ whipping out the money lenders from the temple, it depicts scorn for those who put profit before good. *The Author*

Yorkshire, which in turn owes him a great deal. Originally alarmed by it, he learned to enjoy what he called 'the vitriolic eloquence and robust vernacular of the West Riding'. Asked on one occasion to sum up his own contribution, he laughingly recalled a full meeting of the West Riding County Council in which the Vice Chairman was minuted as

Our Lord Driving The Moneychangers Out of The Temple

Commissioned And Presented By Sir Michael Sadler To The University Of Leeds As A War Memorial to those Members Of Staff Who fell in The First World War. Dedicated by the Bishop of Ripon on June 1ˢᵗ 1923. Its first site on the south wall of the old library was found to be unsuitable and its present home dates from 1961.

Much controversy surrounded Gill and this carving, which included protests from the Yorkshire Post, who tried to halt, or at least delay its dedication. Some reasons for its unpopularity stemmed from Gills decision to cloth his figures in modern dress, and his "implied" suggestion that capitalism results in greed; results in war.

The carving was called by Gill "A sermon in stone" and includes two inscriptions, one on the cornice and the second in the right hand panel as an integral part of the work. A translation of the cornice inscription reads :— "Go to now, you rich men, weep and howl in your miseries which shall come upon you. Your riches are putrid." A translation of the panel inscription reads :— And when he had made, as it were a little whip of cord, he ejected all from the temple and the money of the moneychangers he poured out and overthrew their tables. And he said "Do not make my fathers house a house of commercialism".

The inscription which goes with the engraving. *The Author*

saying, 'And as for t' Education Officer, I wouldn't pay him in washers!' He could afford to smile, knowing that there were, and remain thousands, teachers and learners, who would not agree.

One hundred years after Michael Sadler supported Sam Clegg in opening his world of creativity, relevance and aspiration at Long Eaton, the opening of a new school is proposed to replace it. Just the same length of time that this extended family has fought to better the education of such communities as Giddy sought to stifle. Their educational legacy and successes are as wide as the magnetic geographical and dramatic fields of the Attenboroughs, and the horizons broadly aimed for in Clegg schools and colleges. Principle of action and vocation were their bricks and mortar. What remains to be seen is what 'buildings for the future' will bring to compare with the results of a shared vision of aspiration which enriched and inspired those old coalfield and mill communities. Maybe we can import inspiration, as we now do coal, linen, wool and cotton; and someone will invent a wheel. Or possibly there will be an eruption of new assessment indicators to confirm that the emperor has even more cool and trendy new clothes. Whilst finances and resources are privately and publicly poured into education, education, education at an unprecedented rate, I have to wonder if the 'new' systems, cables and networks, electronic or otherwise, will carry that same 'electrifying and vivifying power.' Or will we again in time, weep and howl and whip the money changers out?

He did have a way with words, that Michael Sadler, historian, academic, visionary, educator, man and patron saint of the arts. But then he would, wouldn't he, because there is no doubt of his northern roots, or his home town; he was born and bred smack in the middle of Barnsley.

2

Ian McMillan

'To be a creative person, you have to be a rounded human being.' So says Ian McMillan, a rounded product of his parents and his early education. His memories of a primary education in the West Riding of Yorkshire are bright, self fulfilling prophesies. 'The days of real teachers who would encourage you to be whatever you wanted to be and didn't just stick your work on the wall, they exhibited it. You could spot a West Riding-trained teacher a mile away: walls full of triple mounted artwork on hessian!' Just talking about being soaked in music and drama, poetry and painting brought back another early recollection: the opening of Darfield's new library on April 1st 1964 and a small person's eye view of the first time he saw; so many books in one place.'

We find a common bond – we enjoyed our primary schools, didn't do well at secondary school and both failed Geography O Level. We are in agreement, there must have been some rubbish Geog teachers about. Not Mr Meakin though. Mr Meakin was the man; the fantastic Low Valley primary teacher who finished every lesson by reading poetry to his class. Mr Meakin took his class outside one day when it was snowing and pointed out everything that they had overlooked; not noticed whilst sliding and snowballing past. Blades of sharp green grass peeping through the snow became, 'Grass coming through like a bed of nails, as a bird flew by . . .' and that was it; Ian McMillan knew he wanted to be a writer. 'He made you feel you could do it, string words together like that; I wanted to be like him. Then one day Sir Alec Clegg visited the school; that man was God. All our teachers came dressed up and he took a piece of my work away with him.' Mentioning the childhood memory to a great fan of his, Lady Clegg, the following week, I saw her make a mental note as she asked which school it was. I knew what she was thinking; somewhere still, in those Bretton archives, there will be the first recorded public work of the Barnsley Bard.

Secondary school just wasn't the same. Run on old grammar school lines to him it meant 'continuous assessment, three pairs of identical socks and buy your own apron for woodwork'. Even that is nearly a limerick as I listen to not just the words but flow, the rhythm, the music; he can't help it, his words just come tumbling out ready formed pre-packed as poetry. I'll bet when he says he'd like brown sauce on his bacon sandwich with white bread and a cup of tea, it's half a sonnet. He held on to the idea of writing through the leaden years, this natural born teaching man of many words.

He would call it doing a stand-up performance, but it's the same thing. He may be reluctant to accept that, comparing the teaching of poetry in too many schools as 'death by boredom or gravity'. He calls it 'the Mastermind of the curriculum,' where you have to sit in a chair with a spotlight on you while you try to answer really hard questions. His approach is different; passionately asserting that listening to someone else's poetry should be as great an experience as writing ones own. He concedes that many people first turn to writing poetry at times of great sadness, even trauma, in life, but believes that is no excuse for making it a heavy subject on a permanent basis. His workshops, school visits and performances certainly are a reflection of that. In short he insists poetry should be taught with enthusiasm and practised with gusto; and he'd make a right go of parodying that I'd wager.

He plays a county level game in great self-mockery, a jolly, self-deprecating, slightly crack-pot Northerner as he talks of his first public appearance. 'We were still at school when we became Oscar the Frog, me and my mate Martyn Wiley. The first folk-rock band in Barnsley; playing our first gig at a jumble sale – and nobody, nobody listened to us.' That would have put some drummers off, but he is made of sterner stuff. He knew it wasn't going to be easy but had made his mind up. He recalls Mr Brown, a teacher with a soft- centred, chocolate-coated voice which you can still hear doing voice-overs on Sky TV adverts. He wanted to speak like Mr Brown, and hedging his bets, told him that he was going to be a successful writer. 'Nobel Prize winners don't come from Darfield, Ian,' replied Mr Brown, letting his voice soften the impact of the message. 'No, they don't, so you would have to move to London,' echoed Mrs Gray. If the drummer heard, he certainly was not snared by it.

He hedged his bets again, staying on at school to take A Levels, just in case, and to please his mum. His mum was 'like a film star when she was a girl,' according to his cousin Harry. He's clearly got some of her genes in the determination that is part of his make-up. She and his father had been pen pals for some years before they actually met, not uncommon in 1943, with a reliable postal service and few other means of communication. In those stark and unrelenting days, when self-sacrifice was the norm and the wireless was the dream maker, they would watch for the mail to arrive, recognise the handwriting and find a place to read the latest letter. Tentatively becoming friends, gradually sharing secrets and for months thinking 'one day . . . .' they lived through their writing making plans to meet. He, a Scottish farmer with a dream of being a sailor, found the opportunity to live it came with the war. She, serving in the armed forces was due to be in Crewe, then the Grand Central Station of the British Rail Network at the same time as he was. You can begin to imagine the anticipation building up through the long wait and then the appalling disappointment when she found she couldn't get the pass she needed to go on leave to meet him. It wasn't an era for insubordination, but with all her senses telling her she shouldn't accept the inflexibility of such an order, she didn't. She went AWOL. Absent without leave, to meet the man she already knew that she loved, and dear reader she married him. World War 2 and romantic as the Brontës and the Brownings.

Ian McMillan knew as instinctively as his parents that Catherine, the girl he knew from school would be his wife. Putting past and present on hold, armed with his A Levels, their lad Ian first went off to do his duty, to better himself at North Staffordshire Polytechnic. That was part of the braver new world and future that most men and women had fought for in WWII. He left with a degree in Modern Studies and an old idea; he still wanted to be a writer, but he couldn't get a job as a poet. He could settle for being a performer though, as that bug was biting. He had become part of the folk club scene and learned to do stand up talking to 'very accepting pub and club audiences'. He met latter-day balladeer Ray Hearne, who paradoxically was inspired by unemployment and collective trauma. Recognising each other's potential, he says Hearne fired him up telling him, 'We're going to start a revolution.' They did too; an audible revolution of folk music acknowledging that with all the old songs they knew there wasn't one about Rotherham or Barnsley. The world was spinning differently and Ian McMillan became to poetry what Ray Hearne is to folk song.

He needed a day job and got one; though found that working on a building site was less rewarding for an ex-student, now nick-named 'Degree'. It is that slow-timing humour of the north which can cut to the quick, or floor you with a velvet-gloved glancing blow, fast and to the point. He could handle all that but it did reinforce his early ambition and added to a growing awareness that he was different; now a badge he has no qualms about wearing. He plays it up claiming people know him as 'that fat bloke off telly who wears terrible shirts'.

Also like his dad, he made the right choice of a wife, Catherine, that Clegg inspired pupil from the same school, had become a Clegg trained primary school teacher, who found immense satisfaction in her work. But his job satisfaction went in 1980 with a recession in the building trade and he was sacked. He worked in the local tennis ball factory and wrote in his spare time. It was with Catherine's encouragement and his parents' that he kept going until he was awarded an £800 Yorkshire Arts grant. It wasn't the amount but the boost it gave him that mattered most and feeling regenerated, his work took off. He co-wrote a play and in 1981 his first book was published. Taking writing workshops for the WEA for redundant miners from Maltby and Rawmarsh, he recalls one who was adamant he could make a career out it. 'I've just been looking round our library and it's all rubbish; 'who'd a thowt yer cud mek a living art o' that.' He was learning the painful difference between realistic ambition and pie in the sky, and considered himself lucky. Invited on to BBC Radio Sheffield's *Saturday Morning Show* with ' . . . .likeminded Rony Robinson, I just loved it.' When the producer asked him, 'Can you make me laugh like that every week?' he said he could. 'If they ask a question like that, always say yes,' he says, and again I hear near perfect cadence in the throwaway answer. It was the right answer for Radio Sheffield and won him a contract which he liked even more.

He is of the stable that believes that radio should reflect the area it comes from, so kept his accent and the dialect on air. 'Capstick was there first,' he says, 'a great comic, but there was room for us as well.' He had the odd controversial call requesting that he 'spoke properly' or my favourite, one saying, 'Tha can't talk like that ont wireless.' He can, he has and he continues to do whenever he deems it appropriate. It has brought a comment or two in reviews which he takes in his stride, good or bad. Mostly good, but I understand perfectly his reaction to one particular Sheffield-bred fifth columnist journalist who described his voice as ' . . . pervading the airwaves like bindweed on an allotment'. The rankle is not personal – it's the regional offence he balks at.

It is also typical of him to tell the story against himself, and in doing so he wins another laugh and this one is at her expense, because one thing is indisputable, his feet were and remain firmly on the ground. That does not make him a plodder and neither she nor anyone should be lulled into a false sense of superiority by the disguise. The man has a brain that works like quicksilver and a wit that that slices through patronising pretension and establishment. Despite a lengthy and creditable Friday night record on BBC Channel 2 this is the man who was introduced simply, if not cynically as 'the Barnsley Poet', when first invited to appear on BBC 1's seriously heavyweight comedic flagship *Have I Got News For You*? Having accepted the poisoned chalice, one which has previously caused other able minds and mouths to fill with dust which they then bite, and which implicitly ranked him as an oxymoron if no other kind, he stood his ground and clearly relished giving as good as he got. Yorkshire relish it was and it gave a wonderful flavour to his quick as a flash fried beefy input. He responds he says best to the wonderfully understated reviews of 'blokes up our street.' When I ask what it is that keeps his feet so firmly on the ground he quotes a recent local critical analysis', I saw thee yapping ont telly again.' We both know exactly what it means; round here it is a slightly wry but genuinely favourable reaction, fluently positive and just short of becoming fulsome. It also hints at what might follow if one gets to too big for ones booits.

But he isn't simply a bi-lingual man who is good, as any on national television and as many radio stations as you can count on both hands, and feet. He loves bandying words; the roots, rhythm and rhyme of language as much as he does poetry and his own dialect as much as any language. When his illness and then premature death robbed both the West Riding and BBC Radio of Tony Capstick, many feared that his integrated use of the wonderfully specific old dialect could be lost with him. No more 'what for?' instead of why, 'upperly' for superior, weather forecasts promising that it would be 'siling it down bi morning' or phone-ins asking listeners 'Wor are you on wi' today then, fettling t'house or just ligging abart?' No more 'mindstyer,' 'laikin' and 'that wind's blowing wild enough to blow t'donkeys off Blackpool sands'. And never again will a parochial reference to a local derby between Wednesday and United be announced on BBC radio as a 'nowt apiece draw for t' Deedahs.' We need not fear. Not only does McMillan continue the practice, he aims to enshrine it by creating a new dictionary of Yorkshire dialect; now that will be compulsory reading for my kids.

I thought I'd met a physical poet when I first watched Ian McMillan on stage. Well he was once described in the *Times Ed* as 'the Shirley Bassey of performance poetry'. He has such agility, a stage presence which has a physical edge, surreal combined with an intellect that is very clever, often cryptic, and always funny. There's a lateral echo of Spike Milligan about him, without the psychological fragility. Either one of them could have presented his incontrovertible argument that Elvis Presley was alive well and living in Yorkshire; because Ted Hughes is Elvis Presley. McMillan's claim merits an expedition led by Neddy Seagoon, Bluebottle and Eccles sailing Napoleon's grand piano straight through the Yorkshire Dales to Mytholmroyd via Skelmanthorpe to establish the fact. Their final conclusion would merely echo his own syllogistically incontrovertible stance; since no-one has ever seen Ted Hughes and Elvis Presley in the same room at the same time, it must be true. Ted Hughes has to be Elvis Presley.

There are few men who can claim to have kept a Darfield accent and simultaneously conjure up subliminal images of both Robert Redford and Paul Newman. I think, with his voice-over in that Persil advert, he's outclassed Mr Brown now, delivering the punch line in a Butch Cassidy and the Sundance Kid spoof. It's in his blood, having a dream like his dad and being a rebel like his mother, that'll be why I am seeing him with new eyes. He's made it into the ranks of the Romantics now too.

His output is prolific and varied, from one night stand up comedy in the territory of new wave or alternative comics on the circuit to the most entertaining Bishop's Breakfast speech I've heard. Newspaper columns of pure puckoon nonsense, or slickly concealed delayed action campaigns are racy or nostalgic as the humour takes him. He is unprecedented as Poet in Residence to Barnsley Football Club, to which his loyalty borders on obsessive, but also held the same position with Humberside Police and Northern Spirit Trains. I am just working up to asking him if that last one is why he doesn't drive, when he tells me about having two driving lessons in his youth, when everybody was expected to drive in the same way that everyone expected to smoke when they were old enough. Nervous as anyone on their first lesson he was even more so on noting that the instructor was more nervous than he was. 'He was dithering, and told me to 'grisp the wheel at ten past two', so I did.' Try it! The relationship broke down completely it seems on the second lesson when he was told to stop outside a church. After waiting alone in the car for some time he followed the man inside to make sure he was alright. He found him standing at the lectern alone and reading aloud from the bible. 'Part of a 24 hour vigil and bible reading programme,' he explained, allaying fears that it was divine intervention he was there to seek. But after waiting for the man to finish his stint, that was it with the L plates for Ian McMillan. Clearly at that stage he had no inkling that his future would include him tearing about the four corners of this kingdom at a time when public transport would be a profit making system rather than a public service. 'There were loads of buses and it was only tuppence from Darfield to Barnsley, so I decided having a car wasn't for me.'

And then comes another of what makes him what he is, 'And, if you're late – it's never your fault!' It's the upward inflection at the end of the line that gives it a Hancock quality. It was always the 'very nearly' that made that one immortal line in radio comedy. 'A pint? That's very nearly an armful!' The flow is a natural gift which cannot be taught and that is why Clark Gable couldn't do it. His delivery of 'Frankly my dear, I don't give a damn,' is said to have been an attempt to draw attention away from the word damn, regarded as an unacceptable curse in days when censorship constrained rather than protected. I think it was less than that.

Ian McMillan needs no such direction or coaching; it erupts from his inner fire of creativity. Additionally, either he is incident prone or he has five dimensional vision, and sees round corners in terms of comic observation as he describes a large boil on a hand, but I'm laughing so much I don't know if it's his or the shaking instructor's. As I leave him I feel like Jilly Goolden nosing out undertones that normal people like me can't taste in a glass of wine. I'm getting a peppering of John Betjeman with a slice of Belloc or is it Lear, a fringe of Alan Bennett and just a hint of Elvis and Ted, with full Doddy body and swirling legs sounder than those on Napoleon's grand piano. And through the alcoholic haze I see a clear definition and it is the marathon man of performance Dodd who is the clarifying ingredient. Neither man is just a comic; both are social commentators in modernised jester mode, so much more than the sum of their parts. Their tools are laughter, comedy and for McMillan, poetry. For both their craft has an element of parody, satire or good old debunking. In his sheer celebration of enjoyment of simple pleasures or exposure of folly and vice McMillan shows himself to be far more than a rhymester. He is a profanity-free zone of cultural entertainment and long may he pervade our airwaves.

3

Brian Turner

There's this 'friendly folk' label stuck on Yorkshire people which is really often a bit of a myth. In some cases it is curiosity concealed to acquire the power of knowledge or information. In a pub I used to visit years ago the local landlady kept a large jar on the bar with a notice stuck on it inviting customers to place their business cards in it. It also said that every month the card drawn out would win a prize of a free meal for two in the restaurant. So for a couple of sirloin steaks she had the 'Full Monty' database of everyone's business, and often home, addresses complete with telephone numbers, as well finding out their line of business and their position in it. Freedom of information, not steak.

Others here have very different reasons for seeming to be friendly with so many strangers. As a child it always struck me how many people my father seemed to know when we were out walking. However far from home we were he would touch his trilby or his cap with a 'Good Morning' to everyone we met. Not just common courtesy I discovered years later when I first went down a pit, 'It's an old tradition; he might be last person you'd ever see' I was told. My mother on the other hand would just nod or smile at people, being used to not being heard or able to hear above the noise of the looms in the weaving mills in Elland and West Vale where she worked as a girl. That didn't mean she couldn't spin a yarn of course.

As she shuttled between her home in Salterhebble and the booming textile mills in West Vale and Elland, I'm pretty certain she would have at some stage worked with, or at least come across another girl called Lily who worked in those same mills. 'Lily Riley, as was, then Lily Turner when she married Lawrence Turner, he came from Morley. She made the best ginger cake you could get; everybody in Elland had her recipe for ginger cake. Lawrence's dad got him a job, like they did when work was hard to get in those days, at same mill as him when he first left school, then they moved to Morley when he got a new job at Low Road, Marley Bottom. He worked there until he got called up; he went into the Army Catering Corps. After his demob they lived in a prefab first but then moved to a bigger house. They had four children, Brian then Robert and then the twins, a boy and a girl. Their Brian was only seven when they flitted and he did ever so well for himself.' And you would probably have been told all of that if you had asked about the Turners in Morley or Elland. That traditional way of passing on family or social history or pedigree detail is just another way Yorkshire people gained the friendly or chatty label. It is both biblical begetting and Scandinavian saga-like in style, and survives still in pockets of the old Viking-settled West Riding. And their Brian did do very well, but he still knows exactly who he is and where he came from.

He has his own strong views about the north and south divide, celebrating it and standing staunchly in his northern roots. His academic training has informed and emboldened his instinct that the two strands of English cooking, like the language, are influenced either by the Vikings in the north or the French in the south. Traditionally, dishes were based on that which could be afforded or were available, and the south absorbed foreign culinary influences. Northern food predominantly remained that which people 'could grow, pick, kill or poach'. He is proudly Viking not Norman, and his research is a joy to read – as preface to his 'Favourite British Recipes.'

Lawrence Turner did relatively well for himself too, with the move to Morley where he gained promotion and was made foreman of the mill. As was the custom as the eldest son, Brian initially shared an interest in his father's work expecting to follow him into the trade, and even won a prize for an essay he wrote after a school visit to a mill. And Clegg's theory of the potential for motivation in school visits comes into play again as I ask him what the essay was about. The title was 'Shoddy,' he laughs and we are straight in to a chicken or egg debate. We are in agreement; the word comes from the name given to reconstituted old wool fibres, to differentiate it from pure virgin wool. Like so many words it originated in the working vocabulary of the working classes but then crept in to common usage; in this case now meaning inferior, poorly made, trashy and even counterfeit. We trot out others similarly absorbed nationally, like 'spinsters', daughters who stayed at home to spin wool in the home before the great wool trade in the West Riding spawned the mills in which they then worked. Those original early 'pieces' of cloth were sold in the large central areas of Bradford, Leeds and many other towns. Historically recorded and most spectacularly still remaining is Halifax's magnificent 18th century Piece Hall. We both laugh at the prospect of today's youth being 'bovvered' enough to write an essay on shoddy, or to follow their parents into a trade, as he tells me that his own motivation in changing direction was in part due to his dad's change of career.

Lawrence Turner's army service in catering for the forces was his introduction to cookery, which he found he enjoyed and was good at. After demobilisation he opened a transport café in Hunslett which he ran until it was compulsorily purchased. Ever hardworking and inventive, he moved on, showing the kind of flair he had as a graphic artist for the Co-op where he had created an orange with arms, legs and a smile to sell off their surplus stock of the fruit. Maybe that is a reason that Brian Turner thinks laterally and continues to take considered chances in his own career. But it was Elsie Bibby, or rather Miss Bibby the Domestic Science teacher at Morley Grammar School who really showed interest in him and made him realise how good he could be at cookery, he says. Because of her encouragement he followed his father into catering and went directly to Leeds College of Food Technology. After three years there he got an ironic final report predicting, 'Brian will never be a cook, but he will make it in management.' Luckily what he would or would not make must have been clearer to others when he went straight on to take up his first appointment – at London's Simpson's in the Strand.

From shoddy to swanky in one move! Even the grand chess masters of the 19th century couldn't have done that; not even there, in what was then the world's most famous centre for chess. Gladstone, Disraeli and Dickens would regularly be found there dining and playing chess. By

A Turner welcome to Turner's Restaurant, Millennium Hotel London for Mel Dyke, Aileen Cook, Tim Dyke and Dean Cook. *The Author's Collection*

Turner time they had been replaced by an equally grand clientele, chess had been ousted, and the place was known for what it still does best, serving the highest quality roast beef and Yorkshire pudding. One fruitless attempt of mine to dine there whilst working at the nearby Consumers Association Head Office in Buckingham Street, left me unfed but informed that ladies were not allowed in its Grand Divan dining room, but were welcome to dine in a 'very pleasant' upstairs room. If I had known that there was a no-nonsense Yorkshire lad on the premises, I might not have so readily flounced out in my early phase feminist fashion. Also simmering at Simpson's was what would become a long partnership between Brian Turner and Richard Shepherd, now the owner of Langan's Brasserie. Within two years the pair had moved next door to the Savoy Grill. In 1969 Turner moved on to Switzerland and the Beau Rivage Palace in Lausanne where he would further develop his skills and extend his knowledge of classical cooking.

That done, and just ten years after starting at Leeds College, he was back in London at Claridges where he stayed until 1971. Then he teamed up again with Richard Shepherd and moved to the Capital Hotel in Basil Street. Within four years they had won a Michelin star, and when Shepherd subsequently left, Turner ran the place for the next eleven years as Chef de Cuisine. He also managed to launch the neighbouring Metro Wine Bar as well as the Greenhouse Hotel in Mayfair as executive chef of both during that period. Briefly taking time to work to qualify as a Chef Lecturer he developed yet another skill, that of teaching his now seriously rated performance of his craft. Now Michelin-starred themselves, Gary Rhodes and Shaun Hill were amongst those who began with him.

In 1986 he struck out opening the first of his own restaurants, Turner's in Knightsbridge, which is a long way from Elland. It may have seemed to be a brave move in a notoriously precarious business, but not to a man still learning as much as teaching. His experience in some of the finest establishments in Europe was adapted to his inimitable personal style to form the basis of the venture. His established international clientele followed him to mix with Knightsbridge locals in what quickly became a high profile 'in place' with the 'in crowd.' Diana Princess of Wales' visits always ensured the most massive media coverage especially on St Valentine's Day . . . A former colleague of his there tells me the secret ingredient was the 'measure of the man himself, that lovely Yorkshire warmth the clients loved; and if he wasn't there they just weren't as happy.' His view is still what it was; his original philosophy that customers deserve and appreciate the best in food, service and personal attention. For him that meant his own attention to every detail whenever possible.

Brian Turner received a Lifetime Achievement Award at Yorkshire Television Studios in December 2005. *The Author*

The next steps were to open the Brian Turner Restaurants, the first over a three year period at Birmingham NEC, and then at the Millennium Mayfair Hotel, Turner's Grill at the Copthorne Hotel Windsor, Turner's Grill at the Copthorne Hotel Birmingham, and . . . watch this space. This stands well enough as an impressive achievement and even a place to ease off, but to it he added the launch of a range of sandwiches, fillings, salads, porridge, Christmas puddings and coffee. His greatest strength throughout remained, the dyed in the wool, no nonsense approach to ingredients, presentation, staff and clients.

Sheila Fitzpatrick worked with him for ten years and throughout that time 'never once heard him raise his voice to any member of staff, or swear at even the worst performing, lowest rated Commis.' Though no longer living in England she tells me that whenever she visits the country she seeks him out. 'He is a true friend and the best people-person I met in the business; the only thing he would never let go is friendship,' says the person who organised his 50th birthday and has just flown back in to say hello for his 60th. 'And as much as creating great food, he is a total believer in education and spends immeasurable time helping young people to learn.' He had forgotten to mention to me that, in addition to a clutch of other honours in 2005 he was awarded a Fellowship of the City and Guilds of London Institute, the British Hospitality Award for the training and development of young people and the Springboard Award of Excellence.

I note with some glee that Turner's passion it now seems is directed at education, and in particular the 'Schools' Futurechef' competition. Like him I can remember those years in the eighties, when cookery and housecraft or domestic sciences, taught mostly to girls, were being dropped from school timetables. Now we contemplate the product of school generations taught the design and realisation of a corn flake box, but have little idea how to feed themselves without take-aways, and think cookery is restricted to using a microwave. We wonder aloud why no-one heeded those pleadings from his profession and mine to teach such survival skills to both boys and girls rather than reject them with the old 'passé' and the newer 'politically incorrect' condemnations. We are in agreement again that though long overdue and another full circle, the latest reports that cookery is to be re-installed as part of the curriculum is good news.

Having only watched him on TV for years as one of the country's leading chefs it's easy to make the common mistake of thinking you know him. I don't think so. He's not one to play at being cool; it's not an image he would be comfortable with. When I ask him if he is acting on TV he says not. 'I think I'm being me, just as I am, but you have to magnify the character for TV so it is me, but done bigger.' I had met him first at the Yorkshire Awards just over a year earlier. We had no idea that he was there to collect an award, this time for a lifetime's achievement of being not only a success in his own right but a credit to the county of Yorkshire. We were lucky seated on the same table as he was all sharing in a delightful evening of pleasure celebrating success, achievement, wit, fun, non-stop laughter and genuine interest in each other's company. It was a coruscating night in the midst of Yorkshire folk enjoying the best of each other's company, and he was the epicentre. He was also the one celebrity there who to my knowledge

Calendar Girls Roz Fawcett and Christine Clancy congratulate Brian Turner on his award. *The Author*

kept every promise of support he made that evening to a host of people seeking it.

He kept the one he made to me and so I find him, despite his punishing schedule, courteously willing to tell me about his life and his work, as his guest at the Food Show at Birmingham's NEC in 2006. I had never been to a Food Show before and find the place crammed but superbly organised. I learn more about both the man and the place as I am escorted through security. The NEC has just celebrated the thirtieth anniversary of its opening, and my escort Mike has met hundreds of the stars who have appeared there and recently became a bit of an NEC star himself, conducting the TV broadcasted tour of the place. He hands me over to Jane, who informs me equally proudly that she has worked there before with Brian Turner, ' . . . but he wouldn't remember, it was eleven years ago.' She recognises my accent so tells me also that she has just graduated in Conference Management at Leeds Metropolitan University this year, on the same day that Brian Turner received an Honorary Doctorate of Science. 'He is great, an amazing man,' but though she was standing close to him at the graduation ceremony she didn't speak to him she says 'because he wouldn't remember would he?' She is right, it is unlikely, and she's wrong, he does remember. When I tell him the tale he instantly adds to it, confirming it was a Domestos sponsored event and had a really efficient team. And she is right again, I find it amazing as he asks for details of exactly where she is located in the vast venue, so he can 'pop down for a natter' if he gets a minute.

I watch him work a crowd of two hundred craning necks and mobile phone cameras as he cooks English beef perfection to further perfection. He changes pace and even his voice to highlight the teaching points separately from his stand-up comedy routine, to focus their attention on learning. Like them I'm amused, and watching a group of young people taking it all in I am also curious. As he finishes I ask them why they are clearly such Turner fans, when there are so many dishy young chefs not much older than them around to see. 'That's the point,' says one, 'he's old enough to have seen it all before, he knows what he's talking about. It's about the food not him, and he puts it across with no messing.' 'And no swearing', says a young girl with him, 'but he's still funny and entertaining.' I blithely feel the two generations between us disappearing in an optimism of shared standards.

He is doing a stint signing copies of his books, but spots Mary Faulkener in the crowd and calls her over to introduce her to his wonderfully efficient, accessible and totally co-operative PA Louise. Mary it seems has had to make the journey from Nottingham alone, due to changes in the original plans. 'I don't like it as much coming on my own, or doing all the driving now but I couldn't miss him,' explains the

Brian Turner and
Mary Faulkener.
The Author

Chairman of his Fan Club. I ask how the club started and she gives me
two versions. Her husband it seems always claimed it was because
she fancied Brian Turner on *Ready Steady Cook* – 'You always want the
Yorkshireman to win.' Her account is that when another 'celeb chef'
said he was too busy to talk to her and friends at a Food Show over ten
years ago, Brian wasn't, 'and we've been fans ever since.' Enthusiasm
grew and with swelling numbers they all used to wear badges at events,
'but he doesn't need that now.'

He doesn't, not when you see the emptying shelves of his other eight
publications and today *Brian Turner's Great British Recipes* going like
hot cakes. But start to take the rest of his working life into account and
it is difficult to see how he fits it all in. Now President of the Academy
of Culinary Arts after eleven years as its chairman, he is regularly invited
as guest chef, judge and demonstrator of great British food at locations
worldwide and is Chairman of the UK Hospitality Skills Board. His
commitment to the London School of Tourism has won him an
Honorary Professorship of Thames Valley University. His efforts in
tourism and training in the catering industry were recognised when he
was awarded a CBE in 2002.

All this is without a mention of what he is probably most widely
known as, a TV chef. It must be an insatiable appetite, or simply a reflection of the silent majority making their preferences, or needs for
television cookery programmes known. Is it a coincidence that the
growth in the demand for cookery programs on television is in direct

correlation to the demise of the teaching of the subject? It seems to me a similar thing happened with Trivial Pursuits and other factual and general knowledge games and quizzes when modern trends then debunked the teaching of facts and figures. His salt of the earth refusal to throw out the baby with the bath water, or to abandon the teaching of basic skills across his specialism, has been an essential ingredient for twenty years or more, not only in the quality of his teaching but also the growth of the TV cookery industry. From residencies to his own series, from 'Master Chef' judge to 'Food and Wine' expert, from Granada to ITV to BBC and Anglia to Carlton, from 'Good Morning' to 'This Morning', 'Out to Lunch', 'Saturday Kitchen' to 'Saturday Chefs', and of course, the compulsive 'Ready Steady Cook'. In fact 'Anything you can Cook' 'Disasters' or 'On a shoestring' or as a 'Mastermind' he's already done it.

As a workload it is enough on anybody's plate, but there are seconds too. When he received the 'The Special Award' at the Hotel and Caterer's prestigious Catey Awards, it was in recognition of his immense and tireless efforts with a number of charities, as much for his commitment and dedication to the British catering industry. I'm intrigued by the diversity and the prospect of some of his choices amongst the many causes he works to support. His contributions to events for the Anthony Nolan Bone Marrow Trust or running the London Marathon for Aids

Moonwalk for Breast Cancer fundraisers: Kate Dymoke, Alison Augsburger, Lyn Cook, Stephanie Watson, Fiona Barnsley and Alison Simpson.
The Watson family collection

Paul Rankin and Brian Turner. *The Author*

victims are fairly easy to visualise, and I can just see him riding at Windsor Racecourse for the Princess Trust for Carers. I bottle out though of asking him what kind of bra he wore when he did the Moonwalk for Breast Cancer, but I silently bet that he wore one.

As the day draws to an end it is time for a live performance of *Ready Steady Cook* and a chance for him to batter his good friend Paul Rankin. They play up the competitive element, but there is just a hint of reality when the secret contents of the famous red tomato and green pepper bags are emptied out onto the tables. He clearly can't believe his eyes when he sees what he gets; a tin of lentils, a tomato, a small piece of beef steak and the biggest bag of frozen peas I've ever seen. Told it cost £4.99 he mutters, 'That'll be 99p for that lot and £4 for the peas then?' Then he fakes a grumble about the sort of peas, 'They need to be marrowfat peas, soaked overnight in bicarbonate of soda before cooking and a bit of butter and mint on 'em.' When told he cannot even supplement the meagre bag by adding eggs or alcohol either because the contestant is pregnant, he hams up an offer to work with his right arm tied behind his back. It's Rankin's affected glee that gives the game-playing away, and of course with a much better choice of ingredients, he wins despite dropping one hot dish on the floor. For the audience it's all a great laugh and of no consequence, but for one poorly little lad sitting beside me in a wheelchair it is just too much.

Throughout the programme the he had constantly called out his support, 'Byan, Byan,' and on realising the result he wept. In the Green Room where I meet up with the chefs I tell Turner of the incident. His reaction is to shoot straight past me back into the auditorium to find the boy. By the time I am able to catch him up he is returning from the main entrance saying there is no sign of him. As we turn to leave he spots the family over by a side exit and runs over to them. I can't hear what he is saying and don't need to; I can see the beaming change on the child's face. It is easy to see why Brian Turner's staff not only like and respect him but have such affection for him too. It might just be why he is the recipient of one very special honour, so rare it is almost blue, and is the only one that he personally chooses to point out to me. The recipients are diverse; Billie Joe's got one but that's not the same thing; the North east wind has a real one, so have Psyche, Mrs Thrale, autumn, the nightingale and even melancholy. With the biggest laugh of a very funny day, with mock gravity and more than a pinch of salt, he proudly announces that he has had an ode written to him. 'An Ode to Brian Turner' is not by Keats, but by none other than the Barnsley Bard himself, Ian McMillan.

4

Pearl Fawcett

I'm told that there are four films which remain loved and acclaimed in the US as being what make people really want to visit Yorkshire. If we discount the Oscars, the best films it seems, include the movie version of Barry Hines' novel *A Kestrel for a Knave*, which became *Kes*. Having had some difficulty in translating parts of the local dialogue in that, Italian first generation New Yorker Catherine Costanzo chooses as favourite the classic original version of *Wuthering Heights*. 'Yorkshire is even better than I remember seeing it at the movies; it's as beautiful as Italy' was the verdict. That might of course have something to do with the film being in black and white, but she clearly instantly captivated as she finally came to roam the heather purpled moors and walk the cobbled streets of Haworth, doesn't think so. Fearing daughter Angela back in New York might never share the beauty of it she picked and took home a promissory sprig of the heather for her.

West Coaster Mary Valentine tells me that *Calendar Girls* does the same in showcasing the beautiful scenery of the Dales. 'It has also done as much to boost interest in the WI over here as well as it has in England,' she tells me. If that is hard to swallow consider this; her Easter plan 2007 is escorting a group of Californian philanthropists to the UK. They will visit London of course, Gloucester and Highgrove, the Yorkshire Dales – obviously to do the Calendar Girls Tour, and finally – Barnsley! Admittedly that is as much because Rita Britton has agreed to open the Clearance Sale Room at Pollyanna for the day to these internet shoppers, but also because Mary wants to share her love of every aspect of the character of Yorkshire.

'We love a parade over here,' I was told by John and Midge Sweet as they proudly wheeled me out to see a great one – the Inman Park Tour's Parade in Atlanta Georgia. 'This band is as good as any in the state.' It was good too, but I'm still not convinced that the band could match up to Maltby Colliery, Black Dyke Mills or the 2006 World champions Grimethorpe Colliery Band. *Brassed Off* is why most people I met in the US keep strong memories of an era they recognise politically, but it's the brass band they really love. They have incidentally kept tabs on it since the film, reminding me that the band's 2006 World Championship win is their first since the one which coincided with the closure of

The Mayor of Barnsley Cllr Margaret Morgan conducts World Brass Band Champions 2006, Grimethorpe Band. *The Author*

Grimethorpe Colliery along with thirty others, including Maltby, in 1993.

Without brass fanfares another world champion, who has also filled the Albert Hall, may now be ready to step back into the limelight. From her first public appearance it was clear that child prodigy Pearl Fawcett would make her mark on the world of piano accordion playing. Her parents had guessed as much when she was eight and they allowed her to use a small accordion on which she taught herself to play *Bluebells of Scotland* with her right hand. Within three months she was being coached on a larger instrument by Barnsley teacher Horace Crossland, and she already knew she loved the work and didn't mind the demands it made. She rebuts the notion of it being a gift. 'I believe it was more of a talent,' she tells me. 'A gift is something you are given without having to do anything; if you have talent you have to work to develop it.' I would argue that she might have both, but am ill-equipped to challenge the only woman in the world to win the Junior World Championship one year, and the next year take the same title at Senior World level.

It must have been hard work too for such an incredibly slight child to master the bulk and weight of the instrument, but master it she did winning every major competition organised by the British Association of Accordionists, including the British Commonwealth Challenge Cup for four successive years. By the age of twelve she was appearing on BBC Radio, and a year later made her first of many TV appearances which continued whilst working for Graduate Teaching and Performance Diplomas with honours at the Royal Northern College of Music. Her achievements there studying piano, cello and all other branches of music are self-evident in her subsequent appointment to teach and finally to become Professor in this same college which had given her immense support as a student. She finds that to be in stark contrast to the response she had received in her grammar school days. Whilst having the shrewd support of an enlightened headteacher who recognised the reflected credit her success would bring to the school, she recalls rather less support from some teaching staff. Oh George Bernard Shaw, were you right after all? 'Those who can, do; those who can't, teach.'

She identifies a distance that she felt was always there, and she knew she didn't fit in with others of her age. At the age of fifteen she had a work load that would have brought down many twice her age. Not only was she rehearsing and taking part in innumerable concerts and broadcasts on radio and TV, she gained a distinction in her Grade 7 piano examination, was awarded another for the accordion diploma and revised well enough to take and pass eight subjects at O level. Her view is simply put, 'If you really want to lay the foundation of any talent for life, there is no short cut; it is work and more work, which you will do if you know what you want and you want it enough.'

Ultimately, though enjoying teaching, she resigned her position as Professor at the Conservatoire where she was the first person to teach

Pearl Fawcett, another World Champion. *Pearl Fawcett's collection*

41

accordion and to give accordion recitals. Her quest to make the accordion an instrument to be taken seriously now assumed more importance, and she decided to concentrate on a career performing. She was identified as having the capacity to become the leading artist in her field by the internationally famed Maestro Adriano Dante, impresario, writer, composer, arranger, publisher, teacher and of course accordionist. Their work together developed into a strong relationship and finally love and marriage which lasted until Dante's death in 2005.

Throughout that time she performed and filled every great concert hall in England including the Royal Albert Hall, Wigmore Hall and the Royal Festival Hall and for ten years was a very popular artiste on BBC Radio's *Charlie Chester Show*. In 1977 long before Glasnost, and five years before Billy Joel, she made cold war history touring the former USSR, the first accordion virtuoso from a non-communist country to do so and therefore the first British accordionist and western woman ever. She treasures those memories of being cherished with flower-filled, foot-stamping applause and receptions in Kiev, Minsk, Leningrad, Tallin, Vilnius and Riga to a mighty crescendo of a finale in the great Tchaikovsky Hall in Moscow. But her dearest memories are of Italy, Dante's home country, where they shared time between tours and a life in London.

So it is fitting that she should be permanently honoured there above

Pearl Fawcett is imprinted in wax. *Pearl Fawcett's collection*

anywhere else in the world, including her home country. In Rocoaro Terme, northern Italy, there is a unique museum which celebrates only those who have most famously influenced the world's players by their contributions to the rare world of the accordion. In 2005 Pearl Fawcett-Adriano was awarded its highest honour: a wax imprint of her right hand was taken to be preserved there in perpetuity. In the select world of accordionists that is the equivalent of a Hollywood hand print outside Graumanns Chinese Theatre. It comes only as the acknowledgement of perfected skill, and recognition of her accomplishment covers the full range of technique and control. 'Her subtlety of expression and split second changes of register have brought a new dimension to the instrument.'

It seems to me that a work ethic is there for life. Having achieved everything she set out to do professionally and for the recent past spent her life nursing both her mother and her husband; maybe she could now enjoy an easy, relaxed life. Not so. 'I need the cerebral practice, it's good for me, but had no idea of trying to make a comeback,' she tells me. Persuaded by friends and fans she relented to play a concert in 2006. A standing ovation with half the audience moved to tears by the performance, and everyone delighted to see her back, had as big an impact on her as it did on them. My guess would be that if you have never seen a virtuoso performance by a world class accordionist, you may well get the chance.

I was an enormous fan of Victoria Wood before she came to live in Yorkshire; since the first time I saw her on *Opportunity Knocks*. *Acorn Antiques* ranks with *Beyond the Fringe* as the funniest things I have seen in the West End, due in part to superb writing combined with comedic acting skills, in this case Julie Walters, Celia Imrie and Victoria Wood herself. Numerically bigger and an equally fine parade of the country's acting talent lined up in her late 2006 TV series *Jam and Jerusalem*. It was with mixed feelings that I had to conclude that this parody of the Women's Institute was farce which bore no similarity to any WI branch I have spoken to in over forty years of doing that. For me the best of it was the beautiful voice of Kate Rusby opening and closing each episode with a contribution of musical originality of such quality that it seemed quite out of place there, but not in Yorkshire.

5

Stephen Smith
Charlie Williams

Question: What do Pearl Fawcett, Seth from Emmerdale and a Rotherham based lawyer have in common?

Answer: Horace Crossland. The piano accordion: former World Champion title holder seems to have taught everybody within two hundred miles of New Street how to play it.

Question: How did people coming to his music shop from so far away, without Sat Nav, know when they were nearly there?

Answer: Moustachioed Barnsley icon PC Bob Harbour, on point duty there for years, would have directed them.

Question: Who's the lawyer from Rotherham?

Stephen Smith, son of a Co-op butcher and with a mother who also had a job, in a factory. 'We didn't have much money but we had some fantastic meals' is his opener. Both hardworking and bright, his parents' misfortune was that they were born too soon. He was just another who missed his chance of a grammar school education because his family's need of the income his job would bring; she was just a girl. Originally from Sheffield, Smith major (or senior really) had served in the Second World War as a Gordon Highlander. He and his wife were real family people, 'They were superb parents, using what little money they had to ensure that my younger brother Neville and I were always well-dressed and well-cared for.' Stephen Smith's memories are of a childhood as happy as his approach is positive. He is a man whose glass is permanently half full. The damp accommodation above the butchers shop contributed to chronic asthmatic croup affecting both him and his brother suffered. 'It meant we got a council house, and moved to Athersley, of which he says. 'You had to be able to run or feight, so I did a bit of both, running being the favourite! I have some fond memories of Athersley though.'

'An otherwise uneventful youth' he says of a normal working class upbringing of the times just after the war. A borderline 11Plus result sent him to a good central school, an educational nesting box between the academic grammar school and the craft based secondary school, where his only unlikely distinction was as President of the Badminton Society. His sole interest from the age of ten lay in playing with Barnsley Accordion Band, of which he eventually became Principal Player on 'first'. For my benefit he adds 'That's the equivalent of leader of the orchestra in concert terms,' in case I didn't know or wasn't impressed, I think. I didn't know and I am impressed, with that and also with his numerous national titles successes. Additionally given responsibility for the comedy input for performances he enjoyed and gained confidence in public performances. The instrument kept its incredibly popularity until the music revolution of the Sixties meant every boy's birthday or Christmas list included the now cooler, trendier, and slightly less cumbersome guitar.

Leaving school with an acceptable though minimum 5 low grade O Levels and no Careers Officer to advise him, the elder Smith Minor made one decision about his future career: he did not want to be a miner. Despite it being one of the popular destinations for early leavers and always an available job, it wasn't for him. Without adequate qualifications he had no interest in university prospects, and he didn't get a job, but did aspire to become a professional musician. Quite by chance his life changed when a friend of his with a job in a firm of local solicitors which had a team in a football tournament said they were a man short. Having been, 'a useful player at school,' he agreed to play for them, turned up and scored three goals which put them into the quarter final, where he scored two more. In the semi final he scored again, four more goals and impressing the senior partner in the firm. He was due to be interviewed by Barclays Bank at the same time as the final was to be played and without him the it was felt the team had less of a chance. Hearing this, the senior partner promptly took an executive decision offering him a job as an office boy in the firm of solicitors instead. He took the job, played in the final and they lost 3-1; but he kept the job.

Well, for while he kept the job. For him it was simply a way to appease his parents who didn't approve of his lack of a job, and it was some-where to work whilst he waited to be discovered as a professional musician. By his own account he did not take his duties as seriously as he might. The Senior Partner had bought a particularly valuable desk originally owned by Lord Byron. Instructing him and a couple of other office juniors to move it he said, 'Smith, take Lord Byron's desk into the basement for storage'. He is now amused at the naiveté of his response

'What's Lord Byron going to use then?' As a small child I was always troubled by the chaos that Laurel and Hardy invariably caused in their films. *Helpmates* is the classic, but I have memory of another, and the two of them trying deliver an upright piano up a long flight of steps to an apartment on a hill. I have an ominous feeling that he is going to tell a similar tale, and he does, but he is funny.

They got the desk into the lift and then, too late, discovered that the width of the opening of lift doors on the basement floor was smaller than on the floor upstairs. 'The desk got stuck' he explains, as if the inanimate object had done that without help from anyone. They carried on following instructions, trying to move the now damaged desk through another door when one of them noticed that an accident prone leg had fallen off as well. 'We were not particularly worried because we thought it was being dumped anyway, so we heaved the wreckage into a corner and dumped it.' Things were fine for three months until a visitor arrived from Sotheby's to value and possibly purchase the desk. Stronger on knowledge of local butchers than he was on London dealers, the office boy initially made a mistaken assumption that Sotherby's was Sutherland's, a potted meat firm in Sheffield, but quickly learnt they weren't. 'In a blind panic I went into the basement with a hammer, nails and the pathetic intention of making good the damage, and found the desk had gone.' His rambling account to the curmudgeonly caretaker brought, 'Who the Hell is Lord Byron and what on earth does a potted meat factory in Sheffield want one of our old desks for?' He then disclosed that he had used the desk to fire up the boilers, all that was left of it would be some ash in the grate of an old wood burner. It was a stark revelation, and an early lesson in telling the truth, the whole truth and nothing but the truth. The footballing hero coughed the lot and was sacked on the spot.

By the age of twenty one he had wandered through a couple more law firms in Barnsley and Wakefield. 'Deciding that the chance of a reasonably good piano accordion player who told a few jokes getting into main stream entertainment was unlikely, I reluctantly decided that a change of direction was appropriate.' He seems to have clocked that he had to work at it in a much more focussed way too as he began to consider marriage as well as his future career. In those days and with his background there was little or no chance of being able to pay for articles to become a qualified solicitor. So he did a variety of courses, attended night school, qualified as a Legal Executive and left Wakefield.

Newly married and based in Rotherham he began his career as a Legal Executive dealing with civil and criminal law. It was a new and relatively progressive firm with an owner whose policy was to employ young people with similar backgrounds to his in the belief that they had something to prove and would work harder to do it. Within the year another Legal Executive joined the firm, Stephen Wilford one of his old Barnsley contacts, and the combination produced the effect I guess his parents had been waiting for. They worked well together whilst doing well for the firm, as he also continued his long hard slog of night school and correspondence classes. He became a Fellow of the Legal Executives, and increasing responsibility led to promotions in quick progression. On becoming Manager of the Crown Court Criminal Section he was dealing with serious crime and the best legal brains in the country. 'That is when my learning really began; I was fascinated by the theatre of the Court proceedings and I admired the Advocates and the idea of living on my wits like them.' He saw the best and the worst of human nature and learned that there was far more to the job than qualifications and academic excellence.

He was thirty and seriously planning now. He needed further qualification to enable him to start up a firm of his own in partnership with his brother, also training for the legal profession, as soon as he was qualified. Given leave of absence he attended the University of Leeds for six months where he sat another examination, known then as 'the solicitors' finals.' He loved the interaction and the depth of the work, but his personal life was roller-coasted then shattered. High on the work, low on sleep, then his daughter was born at a point when he was tied to his studies, consequently she had to take second place which he deeply regrets. Shortly afterwards came a body blow from which he feels he has never fully recovered. 'The brightest in our family, steady and quick-witted with a very gentle and kind disposition' his brother Neville died along with Heather his wife of one year, the victims of a car crash.

He finally qualified in 1979 but continued to learn and within two years had decided he would go ahead and open his own practice. Up to that point he had been steadily 'bettering himself' but now ambition finally entered his thinking. Long term colleague Stephen Wilford became his partner and they set up their own firm. The measure of their relationship is clear as they transacted that in a way no solicitor would advise. Not then and not for almost thirty years since then, has either one of them thought it necessary to have a formal partnership agreement or contract.

The business was successful, so much so that eventually Stephen Smith had to let go of civil and matrimonial cases to concentrate on Criminal Law, which oddly led to another change of direction. Although not involved in the original trial he was later approached by the father of John Megson a Hell's Angel convicted of murder and

Fundraising for the Parkinsons Society in memory of Charlie Williams, in an amazing night of comedy were Bernie Clifton, Norman Collier and Stephen Smith. *The Author*

sentenced to twenty five years. First declining involvement Mr Megson senior's persistence bordering on nuisance levels eventually persuaded Smith to agree to visit his son in Wakefield Prison. He thought he had heard it all before, but left accepting Megson's insistence that he was innocent. The rest as they say is history. With no Legal Aid or other funding he took the case and worked for almost three years before finally proving John Megson's innocence. The book he wrote about the case named the real killers, became sub judice and was dropped by the publishers. But despite not publishing *Hell is not for Angels* they liked his anecdotal style and asked him to put together some of his experiences in a book of his own, and the series that started with *Boozers, Ballcocks and Bail* was born. After the finalisation of the trial of the two murderers the legal situation was thought to be too complex and the publishers still would not publish the Megson story. Nothing short of stubborn Smith decided to study the business, set up his own brand and published the book himself.

When my good friends in Atlanta ask me if we had black political activists in this part of the world I say yes. It is a qualified yes, but affirmative never-the-less. Charlie Williams made the stand with his solitary first contributions mocking racist mockers, debunking bigotry and ignorance in the gentlest way imaginable in pubs, clubs, theatre clubs and finally on national TV as one of 'The Comedians' from nearly fifty years ago.

Stephen Smith was asked to write the life story of his good friend, Charlie Williams and did. It is his homage to the life and work of the great, universally loved comedian with whom Stephen Smith also made many appearances on stage. I sat on a wall outside Marks and Spencer for an hour once with Charlie Williams. Already ill with Parkinson's disease the walk across the precinct had tired him out so I happily volunteered to sit with him whilst his wife, Janice finished shopping. We chatted about the great day we had at the Oaks School in Barnsley many years ago on the first Red Nose Day. First visitor to arrive and the last to leave, he spent the entire day with the children who thought he was amazing. On this typical Wednesday in Barnsley, crowded with shoppers going about their own routine or business, it suddenly dawned on me what a powerful effect he still had on people by just sitting there. One after another they appeared in view; some pre-occupied some miserable, some window shopping and some arguing until they spotted him. Then their faces changed completely and ear to ear grins spread from McDonald's to Littlewood; as I write both boarded up, it's just another bit of a town's past that's gone.

But not Charlie Williams' memory; that is firmly is fixed. Up to a hundred complete strangers walked up to us in that hour all asking how he was, shaking his hand, kissing his cheek or patting his shoulder saying how and when he had made them laugh until they cried. He did a fleeting 'Heyup old flower' mini performance for each of them, making it a day they will not forget. And I'll never forget being in the wash of that massive wave of affection. A jazz band played its *When You're Smiling* way through the streets of the town and into a packed St Mary's Church on the day of his funeral and you couldn't put a pin down in thronged streets outside for smiling crowds who came to say goodbye and thank you. He had earned a special place in their lives by being who he was and never changing his values.

With the exception of re-runs there are few comedy programmes which match the staying power of the humour of those days, nor the quality. All kinds of meeting groups, clubs and societies flourish as people use the remote control to vote with their feet against the diminishing quality of entertainment. It's odds on that if you write any sort of a book you'll be invited to talk to some of them. There are lists at national and local levels of people who do it well. When the Lord Chancellor visited Sheffield, out of the whole range of the most eloquent profession, it was Smith who was asked to speak.

His wit and natural aptitude have made him a big favourite in the north for years and increasingly his reputation creeps south and even into Europe. His acknowledgement that he continues to learn from everyone he meets is typical of the early under achiever. Before I knew anything about him he was recommended to me as a role model to shake complacent youngsters off the couch and into a future. Over the years he has worked tirelessly for numerously charities and with some of Yorkshire's more recent best known names in comedy: Barry Cryer, Bobby Knutt, Duggie Brown, Billy Pearce and his personal favourite Tony Capstick. For three years BBC Radio Sheffield's David Markwell produced the duo in a clever, weekly combination. Serious legal advice wrapped in hey day gags and antics that were seriously funny led the two to invent 'The mini world tour of South Yorkshire.'

His charity work is not advertised but was recognised in December 2006 when he was awarded an MBE. When I ask him about it the story he tells is of another recipient's emotions. A young man, the first ever Downes' Syndrome to receive the honour, who had controlled his nerves throughout the ceremonial, on hearing his own name called out walked

Billy Pierce, another local lad and great supporter of the charity, was also there. *The Author*

50

Stephen Smith MBE after meeting the Queen at Buckingham Palace. *Stephen Smith's collection*

to meet Her Majesty the Queen and totally overcome, burst into tears. Not a dry eye in the palace it seems as The Queen stepped forward and putting her hand on his shoulder told him, 'Young man, you are a very special person.' 'What a woman!' enthuses the man who always had claimed a devil-may-care towards royalty, but not any more. 'She is absolutely charismatic, she has an undeniable aura.' After the investiture, caught by reporters and in a royal flush he was asked by one of them what the Queen had said to him. Aware that it is bad form to repeat the exchanges he told them he had said, 'I suppose a knighthood's out of the question is it?' It was then that he realised that mikes were on and cameras were rolling, 'I had this vision, having just got the medal, of having to give it back.'

A classic example of how a relatively unmotivated one-idea kid can become a human hive of industry with more strings to his bow than an outsize vest, the successful ex-footballer, author, biographer, broadcaster, musician, entertainer, comic, fund-raiser, after dinner speaker and lawyer still has ambitions he tells me.

Question:	Assuming he has given up on the possibility of antique valuation, or furniture removal and storage, what is left to do?
Answer:	He would like to get into the bestseller list at least once; to lose three stones without giving up good food and booze; and to become the first Zimmer-framed media star.

Watch this space!

6

Graham Ibbeson

Being a sculptor isn't what makes Graham Ibbeson a three dimensional person; he just is. Possibly the most complex person I talked to about work, he is also one of the funniest. Most people who make others laugh claim it as a survival technique, a strategy to avoid being bullied as a child. 'My problem was that I was overweight; I hated clowning but it protected me, so I did what was relatively easy,' he tells me seriously. He is taken very seriously now, and isn't overweight, so doesn't need to clown any longer. In fact he flatly refuses most requests to stand up, take the limelight or even to make a speech. That's the first dimension; the intensely private person, who is first and foremost a family man, 'It's about my work, or should be, not me.'

'I suppose I am a bit of a comedian though,' he finally admits, 'only it does sometimes takes me three weeks or three months to tell the joke. Visual art is a very slow process, but humour is a tool I think it enables people to look at themselves; in much of my work through laughter.' This second dimension makes him in my view, the best of three dimensional humorists alive today. I think the real joke is that outside the art world, relatively few recognise his face or even his name. But if you mention the statue of Eric Morecambe which stands in Morecambe, even people who have never eaten shrimps in that bay know what you are talking about. Most will even know that Her Majesty the Queen did the unveiling, and some will add that she owns the first cast of it. Others will tell you that the miniature 'Eric' is now the accepted comedy equivalent of the Oscar or that Sir Norman Wisdom was awarded one, as was Dame Thora Hird. Increasingly, Ibbeson is recognised and acknowledged as the man who bronzed the immortalisation of the golden age of comedy.

I first met him when he agreed to come to an Education Action Zone Summer School I ran in 2000, for gifted and talented children who were from less gifted areas. I was struck then by his natural air of reserve; an inner quality which conversely provides an outer protection. I thought he was serious and shy, but very articulate.

He relies less on presenting verbally I find, and instead communicates his work, through all five senses. There's a laugh about that, as he describes talking to a group of primary school children visiting the Yorvic Viking life experience. His work was explained to them, as the artist who had made thirty of the life size models of Viking men they were looking at. One six year old promptly asked him if he had done the smells as well. 'Just another critic!'

Meeting him again six years later is for the unveiling of his statue of a working miner, which commemorates one hundred years of mining in South Kirby. It is a seriously superb piece of observation and representation, appreciated at every level by the large crowd. Former miners with their families, and historians, civic and other dignitaries have, with the filming crew for his inclusion in YTV's *My Yorkshire*, gathered to see it. They are not disappointed. There is a wonderfully ceremonial atmosphere, in the way that the still close, even though now closed, mining communities traditionally pay their respects. I am moved by the rhythmic combination of brass band, silence, speeches, a march, pomp and banners, remembrance and colourful recognition of such things on this otherwise grey, chill day.

It is a flashback to those years of miners' gala demonstration days. In part, it substitutes for their years of non-inclusion in the nation's Remembrance Day services. As the unveiling of the statue brings the

Graham Ibbeson's
Miner at South Kirby.
The Author

54

music and speeches to an end people stand, observe, file slowly around the base to look from each angle in turn; then just stand again in self-imposed silence before moving away. Another sensation sweeps across the village green, and people blame the chill of the east wind, and wipe their eyes.

Eventually a lone Graham Ibbeson stands there; seemingly unaware of what is happening about him. I sense a strangeness in his reaction, because he this is not new to him. He has had dozens of unveilings, in equally great and good company and including miners' locations before this. The Jarrow March, Doncaster's Man of Coal and the poignant Miner's family outside the NUM offices in Barnsley. I ask him how it feels, but he says, 'I can't really talk about it today. I'm this miner's kid; I feel I was born to do that,' nodding at the crouching miner's figure. It is a magnificent piece of work, 'flawless' I say, but he points out to me that it is anatomically incorrect. 'The back is the most important thing about it, that's where the passion is. Working with picks did that to miners' backs, so to create that feeling of strength, that power, I needed to enhance it. And I had to scar it.' Then it dawns on me, we're looking at someone he knows; and that wind blows through the village again.

When we talk later about his work he tells me he loves that particular piece but was physically tormented whilst doing it. He is lighter about his work now, almost flippant, and clearly never takes himself at all seriously; only his work. It occurs to me again that he doesn't have to do that any more either; not now that so many other people do. His life size work stands at every point of the compass in the UK, from Perth to Bristol, Southampton to Middlesbrough and up the spine through Northampton, Rugby and Chesterfield. His commissions include leading the way by Eurotunnel at Folkestone to Amsterdam, Munich, Stockholm and Switzerland or via the British Airport Authority to New York and Chicago. And for over twenty years he has exhibited across Europe, Asia and the USA.

With a skilled wit he slices any possibility of pretension off his figures, suggesting what he doesn't verbalise. The innocence, or maybe the trivia, of children's arguments counters the gravity of his Scales of Justice; with a mother's dispensation exceeding even Solomon's. And maybe there's a hint of the 'last' of the best of the past, in shoemaking Northampton. Future generations of that industry may be as far flung as an empire was long before the twenty first century. That's the third dimension, what he is actually about; a unique expression of himself through his art, and challenging us who look at it, philosophically, politically and emotionally.

Realising early on in his training at Barnsley School of Art, 'I see things in the round, the two dimensional flatness of drawings gave me no satisfaction. Space was everything, and remains my interest in expressing myself.' Moving on from what was then Trent Polytechnic, his seven year training concluded at The Royal College of Art with a Masters Degree, which he didn't collect. 'It was just a piece of paper, I had what it was worth in here,' he says tapping his head. For a man who does not enjoy speaking publicly, he has no problem whatsoever making a point or lecturing or conducting seminars. He treats any other enforced audiences 'as first year students.' It makes sense in such a specialised area.

He lives and breathes his art, but grows away from most of his work

Graham Ibbeson begins work on Benny Hill. *The Author*

once it is completed. I wonder how he will react driving in and out of Leeds in future if that is the case. Commissioned by Leeds Civic Trust's Betterment of Leeds Man of the Millennium, his Arthur Aaron is virtually impossible to miss, as the tallest statue in Leeds. I find it strange, that he has that reaction when choosing to work in working in such a permanent medium. 'I loved Laurel and Hardy, they were my childhood heroes; but after a couple of years I don't like looking at my old stuff.' He didn't like Cary Grant at all would you believe! 'Not the person,' he explains, 'but the final result. It was too pushed, organised and the backdrop is wrong; it's a bus shelter.'

His mental images take on board the backcloth, the frame in which a figure will sit, stand, run, walk or fly. To him it is as crucial as the features, gestures or stature of the piece itself. The grand Grant reception at the Savoy Hotel, like all trappings of success, was not his style. I think he did enjoy meeting the Queen who laughed when she unveiled the Morecambe piece, and the Duke of Edinburgh, who in artily asking the Queen what she thought of it so far; may have been giving us a clue most missed. He then added that a Yorkshire sculptor in a Lancashire town might be enough to start another War of the Roses.

Despite being in the presence of the Duke of Lancaster, there's no doubt where Ibbeson's loyalty would be then. His first 2007 commission is a living testimony to one of the fiercest front liners in the modern version of that conflict; Yorkshire's legendary, Fiery Fred Trueman. This most feared bowler of his time used to tell an apocryphal tale; of two old gentlemen who for years sat together in the pavilion of whichever ground a Roses match was being played. One from Yorkshire, the other from Lancashire their own game was to criticise and disparaged each other's team performance. Once when both teams were not playing well, a southern voice from the row in front was heard to call out, 'Oh do come on Yorkshire.' The Yorkshireman, tapping the stranger on the shoulder, asked if he was from Yorkshire. On hearing him reply that he wasn't, the Lancastrian then asked if he was from Lancashire. On hearing that he wasn't, as one voice, they told him, 'Then keep your bloody nose out!' Trueman knew about that. Highly competitive, especially in sport, the great east and west counties maintain their warring image. Let any 'outsider' comment or attempt to provoke it further however, and the Pennines disappear as United Northern England emerges.

As Lancashire has its own proud and loyal toast, Yorkshire has its own proud and loyal Society; of which Graham Ibbeson is an esteemed member. Celebrating the strengths of past and present achievers of the county by recognition through its annual awards, it provides sponsorship for educational and other opportunities promotes development and provides a range of activities for a cracking and healthy social life. The 25th annual dinner of The Yorkshire Society in 2006 was held at the Hotel of the Year Award winning, Brooklands Hotel just after the departure of its General Manager, Mark Booth. 'I didn't come into the business to manage actually, I always wanted to be a chef,' but after a spell at Granville College and starting work at the Savoy (in Brian Turner's footsteps) he eventually worked his way back to his roots in Barnsley. Deserting the leafy suburb of Dodworth for Hazlewood Castle and a thousand year old dream location, his hard act is confidently followed by Francis Hindle and a new management team. Nearly three hundred members and guests from all parts of the county accepted the challenge of Brooklands' famous Barnsley chop, all three hundred simultaneously cooked to perfection by Tim Hamer, Head Chef and his team.

Newly appointed Honorary Vice President of the Yorkshire Society, Prof. Fiona Wood, unable to be there in person, sent a video message of acceptance of 'the immense honour' she felt in accepting the recognition of her links to the greatest county on earth. It is the first formal recognition of her work made in this, her home country, despite Australia having given her virtually every award possible. The Society's rapidly expanding home membership continues to encourage the

Lord St Oswald and Kathy Jackson. *The Author*

growth of foreign branches, with nostalgic new ex pats, or generations of long-since settled families seeking out old roots. New branches already established in the United States, New Zealand, Jamaica with others on the way, mean it will soon be possible to join such groups, reminisce and spread the dialect worldwide.

Graham Ibbeson designed and donated new Members' and Corporate Members 'Yorkshire Society plaques which were unveiled at the event by Chairman, Keith Madeley, whose bubbling enthusiasm has boosted membership beyond recognition since he took over. Ibbeson will never leave Yorkshire, but 'From Yorkshire with Love,' is the exhibition tour of 2006/2007 with fervent fellow Yorkist, Ashley Jackson. Taking the county's arts to the rest of the country, the tour is as big a success as could be hoped for at a time when other artists fear the current love of minimalism has created a lull in the market. Chalk and cheese in every other sense the two dovetail perfectly leaving Ibbeson able to avoid the celebrity, marketing, publicity element, which is Jackson's forte.

Graham Ibbeson's later work is more an expression of his own humorous philosophy through his jokes, points of view or flights of fancy. Clever, comedic, outrageous, impish, cynical, sympathetic, astute, empathic, controlled or whacky observations; they are as wide

Carol and Graham Ibbeson. *The Author*

The Doddy. *The Author*

in their appeal as the materials he chooses. From bronze to textiles or lighting, ancient stone or modern fibreglass, steel and multimedia he selects what will extend his meaning or compliment his purpose. The constant theme is his lifelong love of laughter, 'I think I was born laughing'. When you look at the range he has covered, the figures are a record of the best and most diverse of the twentieth century's comedy Ibbeson style, with an occasional flash of Beryl Cook.

By far the majority of Graham Ibbeson's work has been by commission, including this 'Great Comedians' series, and all but Sir Norman Wisdom, undertaken after the death of the subject. It is not unusual for him to include a familiar face in his work; a bit like the

Alfred Hitchcock signature appearance in all his films, but never himself. Involved once in work with a latrine link, he went for the pun; and used the face of WC Fields for a figure – sitting on a WC.

The small figure I hold in my hand is different.

'That man has made me laugh all my life, he is a comic genius,' says Ibbeson as we look at the figure he 'felt compelled to do'. I know the feeling; the same man has had the same effect on me, and on my brother, since we first saw him at Barnsley's Theatre Royal in the 1950's. Unprecedented for us, we went back and saw his act again that week; realising then that we were witnessing the birth of a new, form of comedy. We and millions more have remained fans ever since, in the longest career in British variety history. For most of us our appreciation is our applause. Ibbeson's of course is multi-faceted, personal and unique. Twelve inches high, a cold cast bronze replica oozing enthusiasm and fun; hair, teeth, smart suited to the last button, stance perfect from the view from every seat in the house, fine finger detailed, and complete with tickling stick is the tattifilarious man himself. Ken Dodd starts his fiftieth year of nationwide sell out performances of

The presentation of 'The Doddy' – Graham Ibbeson's 'From Barnsley with Love' personal tribute to Ken Dodd in appreciation of a lifetime of laughter. *By kind permission of Alex Durasow – AD Photography.*

61

The Doddy. *By kind permission of Alex Durasow – AD Photography*

happiness and laughter, at Wakefield's gorgeous Theatre Royal and Opera House.

The smallest theatre ever designed by Frank Matcham, though described by Dodd as ' . . . a shed; early portacabin with a hint of mock Wimpy' is packed as Kenneth Arthur Dodd OBE receives another award. It is one man's appreciation of his work, which Ibbeson describes as his own small contribution of respect for half a century of Dodd's work. 'I'm a child of the 50s; his laughter was a big part of my life, and in forming my own sense of humour.' It is only at this stage of his development, he tells me, that he thought he was experienced enough to tackle the subject. 'I felt compelled to do it, because he is the final page in the history of variety and maybe of real comedy.' And that clearly is the view of the audience if their response is any indicator.

Later in the show it sends Dodd into a discomknockerated appreciation of Barnsley, not only as producing 'greats like Graham Ibbeson'; but as a town of which he still has very fond memories. 'It should have a theatre of its own, you know, funded and like so many towns I play, big enough to bring in the big companies and names to a community that has always loved theatre.' It's a proud moment for the town but even more so for the artist, who isn't there. Predictably he can't face the handing over of the award himself, so misses the thunderous reception it brings from the full house. Then I finally realise this man, so set on avoiding celebrity, doesn't actually realise that he is one. As people ask me how and where they can buy his work, I hear myself saying, 'He's in the Barnsley phone book, under Ibbeson G.'

7

Patrick Cryne

Those who have met Patrick Cryne in passing will tend to see him as quiet and reserved or distant and aloof, depending on the extent of the charity in their own character. Those who know him a little better are likely to say he is complex and changeable. He dismisses any attempt to pay tribute to his achievements by describing his life story as 'born poor and disillusioned, became rich and disillusioned and got out of business to get a life'. He also claims to have few friends and no plans, except to help those important to him to achieve theirs. To get behind what appears to be a defence system, it is necessary to speak to some of the people who can claim to know him well. His long-term personal assistant, Susan Andrew, believes she was worked out how he ticks. 'Patrick appears to be unpredictable, but he is quite consistent in the way he operates', she says. 'Unlike many of us, he is not a people person. Instead he is more interested in ideas and concepts. He will travel miles to speak to someone who has an interesting project or valuable knowledge, but they will be surprised when he next turns down an invitation to a drinks party or some other social event. They will find it difficult to understand how he was so enthusiastic on last meeting and then apparently has become disinterested.' Knowingly, she adds 'the truth is that he will do anything for a purpose and nothing without one'.

Someone who can claim to be a friend is Dave Hancock, a coach at Barnsley Football Club. He says, 'to be Patrick's friend you have to be a friend of his entire family.' They function as a single integrated support unit, the best type of team. Being his friend is like being his brother. We may not meet-up for several weeks, but when we do we just pick up from where we left off, which is just like families operate. It's all unconditional and based on trust.'

To try and understand why Patrick operates on this basis is difficult. He is reticent to talk about himself so you have to get him talking about his family. In this area, his pride won't allow him to remain silent or evasive for too long. His affection for his mother is palpable as he describes her, a miner's daughter, and the second youngest of thirteen children. Any reference to his father and he returns the subject to his mother as soon as possible. With persistence, I glean that his father was a steeple-jack and later a steel-erector, a gifted man who had a weakness for alcohol. Patrick was born in Hemingfield at the home of one of his mother's brothers, but his father's drinking meant that they soon outstayed their welcome and had to move on to lodge with another one of his mother's siblings. This was the pattern until the family was allocated a council house in Wombwell when Patrick was five years old. His father would disappear for months working here or there, leaving his wife to fend for the family by finding whatever work would fit with bringing up two children without support (Stephen was born when Patrick was seven). 'Ironically, we coped better when my father was away', says Patrick. On the occasions when he returned, life was turned upside down by his drinking which took all the money out of the home and down to the pub, where his father would hold court. 'We were constantly short of money and even food sometimes', he recalls.

As they officially had a wage earner in the family, they were entitled to no benefits in those days. Patrick recalls a traumatising event at that time when the local council named and shamed those in rent arrears by displaying names in the Town Hall window. 'Something that would be frowned upon these days' he says, doubtless remembering his mother's distress at seeing their name displayed for all to see and he became aware of the downside of having such an unusual surname. He recalls with pride how his mother set out a plan to end the humiliation by taking control of their lives. She went to the council offices and argued for and won the right to have the rent book in her name by promising to pay of the arrears within a month. This was a rare victory in the days when men had all the rights associated with being the traditional breadwinners. She was as good as her word and took on extra jobs to make sure the Cryne family was never in debt again. She also legally separated from her husband, but never divorced because of her religious beliefs. When her husband became ill with lung cancer many years later she took him back and nursed him until he died.

Patrick went to the local primary school and was in the age group that was the last to take the 11+, which Patrick passed. His mother had put him down for Barnsley Grammar School, but was persuaded in a discussion with the primary school head to send Patrick to the newly-formed comprehensive instead, Wombwell High School. She suspected that she was being persuaded for reasons other than those on which she eventually made the decision. She told her son later that she felt that the Cryne family was stereotyped as unworthy, and that snobbery was behind the arguments of the educationalist. Her decision though was based on putting him in an environment where there would be no glass ceiling, and his worth and value to society had not been pre-judged. A suspicious view maybe, but perhaps held with some justification.

Patrick claims to have been disinterested by much of his school work and instead favoured pursuing educational themes not on the syllabus, which increasingly we regard as an indication of budding individual strength and even entrepreneurialism. Often these alternative lines of enquiry were sparked in the classroom but only fanned to a flame in private research. He reflects that his classmates and most of his teachers must have seen him as largely an irrelevance – a quiet type who contributed little, but caused no particular problems. Some teachers did see something in him and tried to draw him out with differing degrees of success. He recalls that when he got to the sixth form, one teacher noted that he was the only person in his class that she had never seen read a biblical passage in assembly and insisted that he must do this. She selected for him a passage from the New Testament concerning the 'gifts of the spirit', something she saw as a difficult piece requiring expression in its delivery. She asked him to read it through and when he did, he seemingly delivered it as a monotonous dirge, despite his personal feeling that he was being as expressive as he could be. The teacher asked him to practise the piece overnight for delivery at assembly the following morning. The next day, when he was called to the lectern to read, he found that the bible was closed rather than being open at the correct page as he had expected. He panicked for a moment and then instead of fumbling with finding the passage, he delivered it from memory, probably still without any obvious feeling to the assembled listeners.

The teacher later asked him why he had gone to the trouble of memorising it rather than concentrating on getting the emotion across. He told her the truth; that he had never read it again after his rehearsal with her and was able to remember it because of the ideas being expressed and the rhythmic, repetitive patterns in the text. She took him to see the English teacher who asked him to find something in a poetry compendium that he felt he could read through once and then recite from memory. Finding a poem by DH Lawrence which looked to have a distinctive layout, word patterns and connected ideas, he read it once, and then repeated it from memory. Seeing him differently from that point, the English teacher found a new interest in his progress. 3 As including an A in English 'A' Level at a time when they were much rarer than they are today to go with the 8 'O' Levels that he had passed earlier, is worth taking a second look at, I'd say.

Under pressure from the same teacher who had discovered one aspect of his learning ability he was persuaded against his better judgement to apply and enrol at Manchester University to study economics. He left after three weeks, disinterested in the work, but more particularly missing the one significant friend he had found at Wombwell High School, the girl who would become his wife, Jean Ullyott. They had met and become constant companions in his last year of the sixth form where she was two years behind him. On returning to live with his mother, he applied for a job in the administrative offices of British Steel Corporation (Chemicals Division) at Treeton.

'It was a good time', he reminisces. 'I had money of my own for the first time in my life, the freedom to pursue my own interests and a girl-friend that I was sure I would be with for the rest of my life.' Learning at the behest of others was in the past, or so he thought, until one day when British Steel decided to invite all its employees under thirty years of age to take an aptitude test to see if they had the reasoning to be trained as computer programmers as the new age of information technology started its countdown to dawn. The results of the test showed that Patrick Cryne had achieved the top marks in the whole company. He remembers that he was excited at the results, not because of the mark itself, but because the company had previously said it would train the top performers in computer programming, a subject that he had been studying in his own time by reading books and the manuals for the visual record computers that had been installed in British Steel. He was stunned when he was eventually told that he was considered too intelligent for the role of computer programmer, and instead the company would be sending him to university, this time Hallamshire, as a sponsored student to study business and accountancy. For the next three years, Patrick studied subjects in which he had only a passing interest, but at the same time could spend any free time consuming everything he could on computer languages and the design of software applications.

Ending his time at Hallam with business and professional accounting qualifications he resolved that he wanted to marry Jean and work nearer to home so that they could spend as much time as possible together. As Jean worked in Barnsley he decided to get a job there and plan on buying a house in the town. He had expected that British Steel would resist his departure because of the time and money that they had spent in his education, but the entire company was distracted by the downturn in the steel industry and the massive programme of plant closures underway. Patrick went to work in the Town Hall in Barnsley at the time of local government reorganisation and Jean worked around the corner in the Probation Service. They married in the following year and set up home in a new estate off Burton Road – with a view overlooking Barnsley Football Club. A perfect life was in prospect, a happy marriage, a secure job with prospects and proximity to his football team.

In the autumn of 1978 the momentum of life changed for Patrick and Jean and would never be the same again. Deciding it was time to make some improvements to the marital home, they planned to add central heating and a garage. There was a job promotion opportunity available within the Town Hall which offered not only improved earnings but a more interesting role and the opportunity to work more closely with computers. He applied expecting to be successful as he had prepared well for the interview. Instead, he was told that he had been unsuccessful and should not expect any further promotions. 'When I asked why, I was told that I needed to have the potential to manage teams and, they felt whilst I was talented as an individual, I had not shown the personality traits of a manager.' They had decided that there was no room at the top for someone who wasn't a 'people person'.

In a spontaneous decision to leave the Town Hall rather than accept 'their limitations on my life' he broached the subject with Jean who supported him without reservation. In deciding what to do next he remembered his time at Hallamshire University and the opportunity it gave him to use the library and the computer department for his own personal research. Unsurprising logic led him to take a job at Huddersfield University where he spent much of his spare time in the computer department talking to the lecturers and using the computers for his own knowledge development.

The University of Huddersfield showed the same astute foresight in 1978 by appointing Patrick Cryne as it later showed in appointing John Tarrant as Principal and Patrick Stewart as Chancellor. The big difference was that whilst Cryne's experience was not entirely helpful; Stewart had been given exceptional support. On being appointed University Chancellor in 2002 Patrick Stewart's first action was to recognise that support. Conferring an honorary degree on Huddersfield born RSC actor and director Gregory Doran, Stewart, who had actually dropped out of school to attend rehearsals in his quest to be an actor, cited one of his former schoolteachers Cecil Dormund. It was Dormund who on first hearing the now internationally recognised actor read Shylock, said, 'You're good at this Stewart, you should do it for a living.' Convinced in his judgement the committed teacher then set about ensuring that the boy's potential was not wasted. 'It was down to him' claimed Stewart publicly conferring both the honour and the credit for his success.

Patrick Cryne on the other hand was entirely self-motivated. Absorbing all he could, he then moved on to London to work at City University, again largely to access the best facilities to enhance his computing skills even further. Jean followed him without question despite the obvious culture shock of a move to the bustle of the capital. She recalls, 'we sold our home in Burton Road for £15,000 and found that the cheapest equivalent home anywhere near the city cost £35,000.

In our first few months in our new home we had to adopt some serious cost control measures like keeping the lights off, turning the heating down and eating economically to avoid going into debt, but very soon Patrick was getting promotions and the financial pressures eased.' For their first few years in London, they travelled back to Barnsley each weekend to spend time with their families, and of course to watch their football team. Later, home visits remained frequent but less regular and it became easier to start watching Barnsley's away games because there was often less travelling involved.

In 1984, Patrick decided that his knowledge of modern computing techniques was as strong as anyone he had ever met, even though he was working in a top teaching and research organisation, and decided he would put it to the test. He had seen recruitment adverts for technologists in the management consulting practice of Peat Marwick, then the largest firm of accountants and management consultants in the world. He knew that if he wrote in, his CV would not have the evidence of practical experience that they would require so decided to go directly to their offices to ask for an interview. In late August, he walked into Peat Marwick's headquarters in Puddle Dock, opposite the Mermaid Theatre, and asked to see someone regarding a job as a management consultant in information technology. A somewhat surprised receptionist called the relevant department, and after a while a senior manager appeared with the intention of explaining that Patrick needed to write in sending a CV. Patrick stated his problem was that whilst his knowledge of current computing was as good as the best, his practical experience lagged behind it. The senior manager was still intent on politely seeing him off the premises, but Patrick asked for five minutes to prove that he knew more about the computing and information technology than he did. 'I'm an expert in local area network topologies', said the man. 'Then I definitely know more', came the reply.

Intrigued, the senior manager took Patrick to his office to test the claim. After appearing satisfied, the man called some of his colleagues in to test him in their particular competencies. He was next taken to see a partner of the firm, who also tried out Patrick's knowledge of software applications. Beneficially, this subject above all other areas was Patrick's real interest and where he was both knowledgeable and hungry to know even more. The outcome was an offer of a job, there and then. Asked what level of salary he was looking for he gave what he thought was a reasonable figure and saw the assembled faces looking querulous. 'Too much . . . .' thought Patrick. In reality, he had asked for much less than the company normally paid to its management consultants, and when handed the letter offering him a job, he noted that they were proposing to pay him more than his suggestion.

Patrick's career was meteoric within Peat Marwick. Within five years he was admitted to the partnership and he was working on some major computer projects for the government and major multinational companies. In due course, he decided to return to the north with the firm to be closer to the wider family and, of course, his football team. The nearest major office to Barnsley was Manchester so he moved there and Jean found them a new home in the High Peak of Derbyshire. In 1993, their son James was born – an unexpected, but welcome arrival to parents in their forties. Family life had an important new dimension and business life continued to be stimulating for Patrick.

As the year 2000 started to loom and the potential problems of the 'Millennium bug' in computing was being mooted. Patrick was sure that all of the predictions for widespread computer failure, with planes falling out of the sky and other extraordinary forecast events were nonsense. His own firm started to work more on defending computer systems from these potential doomsday scenarios, but Patrick wanted to work on systems development and new innovations. The result was that he decided to 'buy-out' the business unit where he spent all of his

'Match Day' By John Wood

time, and he set out with like-minded colleagues to make it happen. When the year 2000 finally arrived his new company had been bought out and listed of the London Stock Exchange making him a multi-millionaire. He grew progressively uncomfortable with the corporate lifestyle which required a lot of his time for non-productive purposes, by his definition, and he eventually left in 2005 determined to find more satisfying things to do.

An important project soon came along when, along with the local council, he bought Barnsley Football Club's ground to prevent it falling into the hands of property developers. Later he intervened again to stop the club going into administration when Peter Ridsdale found it diffi-cult to raise the necessary fund to keep it operating. With the valuable involvement of Gordon Shepherd the club saw financial stability achieved in 2006 and a promotion to the highly competitive Football League Championship. Patrick also works on conservation and enhancement projects in the High Peak, restoring wells and public parks. He is also involved in charitable projects in health and education in Manchester and Barnsley. Above all, Patrick is relishing the time he can now spend with Jean and James in what he terms 'family projects.' So maybe somebody was a bit off the mark and Barnsley got that early bit of team selection wrong. He is a 'people person' where it really matters.

Barnsley's sporting history in general, and football in particular, is well chronicled, and the media has consistently reported on former heroes and the credit due to many of the great individual characters. Dickie Bird gained his reputation as an umpire but has retained it as a sound role model in public life and civic duty. A lifelong supporter of Barnsley FC, he is not just a VIP at play offs, but buys his season ticket and is a regular at matches. 'I've had to miss a few this season,' he tells

Dickie Bird. *The Author*

Legendary Yorkshire and England batsman, Geoffrey Boycott is now also regarded as a great commentator on the game. Here, following an impromptu coaching session with fans India, Benny and Mimi Watson. *Peter Watson*

me on returning from the Cricketing Legends Tour played on the beaches of Perth Brisbane and Sydney. 'Sport has given me a really great life and I hope this will do the same for other disadvantaged youngsters,' he says describing the purpose of the Dickie Bird Foundation. The foundation's backing covers other young sporting talent across athletics, golf, trampolining, tennis, ice-skating and of course, cricket from the first award given to an already 'up' and coming young jockey Andrew Yoxall, from Grimethorpe.

I'm keeping an eye on him in case he ever rides Arsene Rupin. That's the horse which beat the best 4 year olds in Europe, as well as horses specially flown in from Arabia, to compete for the first time in the Arabian Derby at Newmarket in July 2005. The win put his trainer, Barnsley born Georgina Ward, into the record books too, as the first British trainer ever to win that honour, before he was snapped up by a shrewd owner in Dubai the following March. She follows a tradition of local trainers including Steve Norton, and Sandra Cooper formerly of Noblethorpe Hall but now York based. If we add the Whittaker family, Steven, John and Michael with twenty years or so of show jumping achievements and then include the next generation we have a stable to be reckoned with in Silkstone. From her early 2001 international selection, to darling of the crowd status 2005, Members' Personality of the Year young Ellen Whittaker is already a force to be reckoned with, and as highly rated in the US as in Europe. As a riding family, the Whittakers raise not only the bar, but the tone of equestrian standards and reputation. With younger brothers Joe and Thomas set to give chase, our prospects for the Olympics look to be in good hands.

Mick McCarthy, immensely popular as Reds' captain, was better loved than Guinness with his historic achievement, taking Ireland to the final of the 2002 World Cup, following an unbelievable run of nineteen wins out of twenty matches. Danny Blanchflower, live on air, became almost as famous for declining Eamonn Andrews' red book and refusing to appear on *This is Your Life* as he was for football. Encouraged by his mother, who played centre forward in a local Belfast ladies' team, he played first for Belfast side Glentoran before signing for Barnsley in 1949. His reputation as a prime mover in proposing that practising with the ball was crucial in training rather than the restrictive system of only physical exercise began then, before his glory days as Spurs captain. Barnsley fans would have forgiven then Barnsley FC manager Angus Seed, the man who signed George Robledo to play for Barnsley almost anything. The story goes that Seed's response was that if they were deprived of ball play in training sessions, 'players will be hungry for it by Saturday!' Twice named English Footballer of the Year, Blanchflower captained Northern Ireland in 1958 when they reached the quarter finals of the World Cup.

George Raynor's name isn't as well known even in Barnsley, though he began his football career in Yorkshire playing for Elsecar Bible Class before turning professional. Towards the end he was just another sacked manager, in his case from Doncaster Rovers. But in between, he was one of the best international team managers the game has ever seen. Just two years after he took over the Swedish national side, they won the 1948 Olympic Games title. In 1950 they finished third in the FIFA World Cup, and took bronze in the 1952 Olympics. As national manager he again assisted Sweden in securing its greatest footballing achievement; a place in the final of the 1958 FIFA World Cup. Losing that title they went on a year later to become the second side to beat England at Wembley. Sixty years after Raynor started his successful career with Sweden, a Swede was ending his as England manager and I wonder if credit for a young Sven Goran Erikkson's interest in football was first inspired by the skills of a Yorkshireman who once played for Wombwell and Mexborough.

Cryne talks of an Oakwell statue to commemorate Tommy Taylor, another signing by Angus Seed and now rated as one of the three finest

Tim Dyke with his grandfather Benny Robinson. *The Author*

centre forwards ever. 'Bobby Charlton says that he was asked to change seats with Tommy who was nervous about flying, and didn't want to sit in the seat he was allocated. That saved Charlton's life, he was one of only 21 survivors in the 1956 Munich air disaster which decimated Manchester United's successful young team of Busby Babes,' Cryne tells me. Mark Jones, never actually played for Barnsley FC, but his name was immortalised through his tragic death in the same crash.

A former Chairman of Barnsley Football Club, the man who personally paid for the original Football League Cup and whose name it still bears, is former President of the Football League, Sir Joe Richards. Local match officials have played their part too. When Arthur Ellis refereed the 1950, 1954 and 1958 World Cup Finals my mother always said that like her, he came from Halifax. When he later appeared refereeing on *It's a Knockout* my dad said that clinched it. It is not a job for the fainted hearted, refereeing; but Harold Hackney, Keith Styles and Dave Phillips President, Chairman, Treasurer and Honorary Lifetime Member of Barnsley Referees' Association have all made immense contributions in their own way to the beautiful game at every level. I have to tread very carefully here since one of my personal favourite refs is Trelford Mills. (The problem is I have a niece in Brighton, but I also have a son-in-law, who is a born and bred fervent Newcastle fan. She might not know about it, but he will definitely remember 1983, an FA Cup match against Brighton when two last minute goals by Newcastle were disallowed by the referee. I can however affirm without fear or favour that Trelford Mills is an excellent after dinner speaker.

In 2002 football's governing bodies took the decision to initiate a new system for the evaluation and appointment of match officials. It was to be a transparent process, merit driven and leading to the best officials being appointed to referee future top matches. The consultant employed for its organisation was a former Barnsley referee, Tim Dyke and the man who is now running General Manager of Professional Game Match Officials Ltd, Keith Hackett is from just down the road, in Sheffield. It's like Mick McCarthy always said, 'If you want it doing, you get somebody from round here.'

David Topliss, former Captain of the Great Britain Rugby League team, donates a signed montage depicting his career to Barry Eldred, Chairman of Barnsley Building Society, in support of the Yorkshire Air Ambulance 2007 appeal for a second helicopter which enables an average ten-minutes response cover of the whole of Yorkshire. *The Author*

8

Hudson Taylor

If it isn't religion that is the spur, it's often politics. Left, right or centre, traditionally mills, factories and mines were breeding grounds for public speakers since the Luddites. A Royds Hall scholar, before becoming an Oxford double first, Harold Wilson was from the heart of Huddersfield. One of the brightest modern parliamentarians, he used his sense of humour enhanced by an impressive memory to reach the public. It may be that Bernard Ingram is one of the ablest politicians from the West Riding textile region. A powerful speaker himself, democratically unelected, his position nevertheless gave him access to the ear and the voice of a prime minister. To be the trusted weaver of such dreams, spinning the public web of private policy, is as influential a seat to hold as any; and more than most on the back benches.

You could tell when he was nobbut a lad at Wath Grammar School, long before Magdalen, William Haigh was a natural; with staying power. Intelligent, wry, funny, prepared and now fully experienced in levelling his delivery to his audience. He is one of few, entitled first by loyalty, then by probity and achievement to poke gentle fun at his home county. His brief absence from the centre stage of centre right politics became a blessing which delighted breakfasters, lunchers and diners internationally. Watching and hearing him speak suggests that amongst his favourites may be recounting wry, anecdotes of Yorkshire election campaigns to Yorkshire audiences. They understand, and share the joke in the manner in which it is intended, the way that families share and re-tell the best of memories of faux pas and bon mots.

At local politics level Leader of Barnsley Council, as we speak, Steve Houghton could walk away from Edinburgh any August with a fistful of awards. His initial delivery is understated, so the rapier wit cuts in unexpectedly, pointedly cogent and ranking above many who have won acclaim there and in Westminster. Now a much sought after dinner speaker, he has mastered the art of coating a political pill with punch lines so easily swallowed that the only pain is from laughing.

You must have heard one of those jokes, about people moving from the south to work in the north of England, as missionaries; especially in Barnsley. We do laugh as we cherish old chestnuts like that; they are virtually all that remains of political incorrectness. The real joke is that since Hollywood chose Ingrid Bergman to be Gladys Aylward in *The*

Inn of the Sixth Happiness little is known of the work of one of the greatest missionaries to China. Such selectivity is not new, but it is comparable to Florence Nightingale's reputation, in comparison with that of Mary Seacole.

May Day Green in Barnsley was part of one of the oldest and biggest open air markets in England in the 19th century. Opposite, on the wall of a pharmacy which once stood there, used to be a plaque to indicate of the eminence of a man who was lived there. They've all gone now, May Day Green, most of the market, the building opposite, the plaque, the man, and for most people even the name that was on it, Hudson Taylor. But a young GP and acupuncturist in Mapplewell now tells me that his family's and his own Christian faith were inspired by Taylor, and the strength of his ministry is what brought the young man from China and with his own family to settle in Yorkshire. I find it sadly ironic that the missionary's name was recognised by few in his home town a hundred years after his death, when a Christian delegation from China came to show their respect for the great man who founded the China Inland Mission.

Devout Methodists, Hudson Taylor's great grandparents James and Betty Taylor despite being ridiculed, abused and despised for their 'new' religious views had welcomed John Wesley himself to their home at the top of Old Mill Lane. There together they held the first Methodist Church in the House meeting, in the town Wesley then described as 'famous for all kinds of wickedness.' Their persecution may well have been the reason for that visit, but the outcome was that James Taylor's faith was so strengthened that he went on to play a part in the building and opening of the town's first Wesleyan Chapel in Pitt Street. His eldest son John, who worked in the town's then flourishing linen trade was equally devout, as was his son James who, though with ambitions of being a doctor, had to settle for the less costly training of an apprenticed chemist. The precise nature of his training in pharmacy was applied to every aspect of his life, as was the honesty and integrity born of his religion. The combination of these assets led his fellow townsmen amongst the group of founders of the Barnsley Permanent Building Society to appoint him as its first manager. It was this James Taylor who having married former governess, Amelia Hudson, the daughter of the Wesleyan minister, gave his first son the names James Hudson Taylor.

The spiritual training, loving care and a meticulously organised upbringing by his parents resulted in Hudson Taylor having an unshakeable faith in God and a resolute determination to do his duty. From the age of four or five he would say that one day he would go to China and be a missionary. The first Protestant Missionary Atlas of the World was published, when he was seven, but it contained no map of China.

For him that was the first spur and though originally a delicate child tutored at home, he continued his studies whilst working in his father's business, learning Arabic, Latin, Greek, Theology and Medicine, along with a growing lifetime love for Botany. Briefly working in a bank in Barnsley and then further years in his father's business, he also trained as a doctor's assistant before finally, in 1853, he sailed for China, answering what he fervently believed was a calling.

Despite initial rejection, and through years of assassinations, riots, famine, wars and the deaths of his first wife and four children, he fought for fifty years for China to know Christianity. He used his frequent journeys home and back to China to draw support for his mission from Canada, America, Denmark, Norway, Sweden, Germany, France and Australasia. On what would be his final arrival in Shanghai in 1905 he was welcomed and recognised as a veteran, and honoured for his wisdom, bravery, endurance and faith.

It was a different kind of brave decision David Hope took as the last twentieth century Archbishop of York; to give up the See of York and return to the roots of his personal faith. His low profile only masked from the casual observer the strength of the part he had played. My first personal memory of him was in 1988, when he gave sturdy support for the 150th anniversary Remembrance Service for the children of the

The Bishop of Manchester and Her Majesty's Lord High Almoner.

78

Huskar dayhole pit disaster in 1838. Lord Mason of Barnsley supported that, and together with Lord Lofthouse of Pontefract also supported the widely held public view that an ideal candidate as the new Archbishop of York would be the former Bishop of Wakefield, Nigel McCullough. Now Bishop of Manchester and Her Majesty's Lord High Almoner, his immense support, especially for children of the dark days of the pit closures earned him the respect, gratitude and affection of the whole of the coalfield communities. His own achievements were simply his faith put into action through a steadfast personal philosophy, shared with Hudson Taylor, 'There is no dream that must not be dared.'

9

Jane McDonald

If you were asked what your dream holiday would be, I'll bet you'd be with the majority – on a world cruise. In today's show business world, without the training grounds and opportunities of the wonderful old music halls, and more recently the equally productive theatre clubs, the dream job is working on a cruise ship as an entertainer. There, weather permitting you can learn the ropes doing what you love and travel the world at the same time. In the days before the unreal reality shows of today, what was considered to be family entertainment actually entertained, and was suitable family viewing. Ten years ago one of the first reality TV programmes *The Cruise*, covered every aspect of life on board, a vicarious experience of cruising. Sadly much of the fresh and innovative promise of the genre has been lost in an escalating inferiority of followers with contrived confrontation, attempts to shock, expose or match make. The outstanding highlight of that original series, on the right ship at the right time was a young woman who thought that she had achieved her dream then.

What remains of that series is Jane McDonald. A laser-lit, sequinned blue figure, she torches onto stage with *You don't have to say you love me* to a crowd which clearly does. It's a dramatic entrance, playing her in own neck of the woods at Sheffield City Hall towards the end of a national tour. Following straight into *I only want to be with you* she's a bouncy '70s mover, complete with high pitch-perfect squeals. Then as she speaks for the first time, 'Oh hello' it's a downward inflection, instantly recognisable local accent that has them answering as she asks them if they've seen her mother in the foyer. 'Buy a CD off her will you, she's working to pay her catalogue bill off.'

It's the beginning of an equally perfectly pitched routine in which she switches from the professionally perfect to sending herself up and they love it. She sways into *Give me time* and then turning her back on them strikes an exaggerated pose, which works, followed by an outrageously sensational bump and grind before turning round grinning, 'I've always wanted to do that!' For anyone in doubt it's now becoming clear that she is also an actress of note, but one who can't resist going back to play herself. She flies through *Walk on by* rumbas her *Way to San Jose* and begs a *Little Prayer for me*, before equalling any previous performance of *Always something there to remind me*. Now she morphs into a loose woman and gives the limelight to her backing group by protesting that she won't on principle ever do that, 'Why should I? They're half my age and both have flat stomachs and . . .' she points to her own chest indicating that it's padded, 'Like spaniel's ears if I didn't,' she claims. They are Yorkshire girls too, ex Intake Performing Arts College and 2005 BBC *Strictly Dance Fever* winner Sadie Flower. Singer, dancer and choreographer on this tour, with a mounting track record of charity events, workshops, summer camps for children and teaching she has been doing since the age of seventeen. Kelly Sneade left the West End and *Saturday Night Fever* to join the tour.

It's a clever move not being too clever, because now she is moving into songs she has very cleverly written herself. There isn't a single person in the auditorium who doesn't understand and feel the tension when she starts with *If I knew then* and carries on straight into *Shades of Black*. We know we are in a part of her private life and it's raw, but she knows that too so lifting it again she starts to sway, this time without moving her hips, and blames it on the Bossanova. The next song she says is 'cheesy if you like, but it's for you, you got me through the worst time of my life' an emotional strike which hits the target even before a voice that is too big for her small frame sends another frisson right through the place. With no hint of belting it out, it's the best rendition I've ever heard of *You're My World* before she slaps straight back into stand up, telling us how she loves touring and playing so many different theatres; but if were not for Emmerdale she'd never get any fresh air.

She gets her breath back with memories of seafaring days on board compared with a happy early life in a landlocked West Riding. More wisecracks 'Those were the days when smack and crack were what you got from your Mam if you didn't behave.' Then, a month before *X Factor* and the full squad of talent did their medley, even with Bjorn coaching, she does it better. Abba condensed into a first half finale of *Rich Man's World, Man After Midnight*, the ubiquitous *Dancing Queen* and a *Waterloo* that certainly isn't one for her. We are left wondering how she will better it after the interval, but we should know by now.

There is more, changes in style, dress, movement, and choice of songs in which I realise that she is taking on some of the biggest names in the business and singing their songs, but they're her songs tonight. Her hips ensure new sex appeal in *Walk on By*, hair shaking and shining does as much for *Kiss me Honey, Honey'* and *Don't Rain on my Parade* gets a new husky Red Hot Mama touch that Sophie Tucker would have been proud of. It's a black tie, red satin sheen that she ends with and then wipes straight off, 'This isn't lip gloss you know, I've just had a bacon sandwich . . . .' She takes another moment to relax a little, flirting with a man at the front telling him 'I want you to leave here thinking you've been tangoed' then sings tango, salsa and rumbas'. We can feel a wind up to a finale as she *Dreams the Impossible Dream* and see the picture of a life like any other, of dreams and fantasies, but all come true. Love plays an amazing and overt part in it for her, and she identifies different love themes and what is constant in her life by dedicating the last one, *The Hand that Leads Me* to her Mother.

Then she does what I doubt many could have predicted as the finale and few would do. She gives the stage up to 400 amateur singers who have come together as *Sing Live UK*. It looks like an anti-climax but how wrong can you be. They do a breath-takingly soaring performance of *Love Lifts You Up* before she is back, changed and singing with them for the real finale. The girl from the cruise has grown up; she's more versatile, sophisticated but looks ten years younger. The whole audience is on its feet and I note that there isn't the usual rush to get out, everyone stays as long as she is on stage and then still stand around. As we leave there must be two hundred of them quietly waiting in the foyer and sure enough in ten minutes she is out joking and laughing and signing auto- graphs and programmes for people, most of whom she seems to recognise or know by name.

The next time I see her she is at a Charity Dinner at Brooklands Hotel. Amongst other local goodies and World Brass Band Champions, the ninety years old in 2007, Grimethorpe Band. This time she is helping to fundraise for the Mayor of Barnsley's nominated charity, Barnsley

Jane McDonald – The Finale. *The author*

Francis Hindle, General Manager welcoming Jane McDonald to Brooklands Hotel.

District General Hospital's Enhanced External Counter Pulsation Unit, chosen after successfully treating the Mayor's Consort, Gordon Morgan, for Chronic Angina. It is an excellent night organised virtually single handedly by Derek Carpenter with the backing of eight generous sponsors, and Jane McDonald is persuaded to help with the auction. Fast not loose, she is slick and funny as she charms the bidding up seriously boosting the amount raised. I win a trip to Galaxy FM to see Hirsty live on air, so it's good result all round. As we leave she is chatting to the hotel staff thanking them, and telling them that she has just finished filming *Loose Women* and is about to take a break. She's going to take her Mum – on a cruise.

11

Joann Fletcher
David Moody

Have you ever wanted to have one of those DNA swab tests that can tell you who you really are? I started to wonder how far back my line could be traced some years ago when I took part in a TV series in which a few people were brought together to discuss various topics from the week's news. We were a pretty disparate set, including one forceful young man who, validating his English origins sought to prove it announcing that his family 'came with The Conqueror' (aka William the Bastard of Normandy). A gently assertive but clever young cleric disarmingly quipped back, 'Really, I'm from a family of Celts; do you think your family will settle here?' It was one of those enviable Oscar Wilde moments, and I wish I had said that.

Like most people I guess, I don't really know who my forebears were or where they came from. Surnames are good clues, often including information on the family's early status or occupation. So Joann Fletcher can make an educated guess that at least one of her forebears was an arrow maker; but from the quality of her love for her home county, I have no doubt he was on our side at Agincourt. She is occasionally wont to demonstrate an atavistic two digit reaction to stuffiness, which might just support that theory. As you would expect in any Barnsley family she has mining links, but for at least three generations there have been hairdressers too. It's an interesting combination of family history that could beg the question of how genetically influenced we are by what our forebears did, since she had no thought of the links in her family history when she made her subsequent career choice.

She flies in the face of every convention normally associated with her chosen field archaeology which, by tradition if not by definition, normally comes with a dusty label. I find her to be yet one more child who was advised that she should think again as her career decision and expectations were not realistic. 'You are too you,' she was told on one occasion. To become an archaeologist even in the 1970s she was repeatedly warned, one had to be scholastic enough to be accepted at one of 'the better' universities, be conventional in appearance, speak the Queen's English, and most importantly be male. She wasn't the first. Barnsley-born, Holgate Grammar School and

Cambridge educated poet, Donald Davie shared a similar sense of place.

His academic and teaching career took him from Trinity College Dublin to the University of California and back to fellowships at Gonville and Caius Cambridge. He was Professor of Literature and Pro Vice Chancellor at the new University of Essex before returning to the US as Professor of Literature at Stanford. In 1987 he was named Fellow of the British Academy whilst first Mellon Professor of Humanities at Vanderbilt University in Tennessee.

His 1974 series of poems *The Shires* contains *Yorkshire*, with a subtitle 'Of Graces';

> The graces, yes – and the airs! To airs and graces
> Equally the West Riding gave no houseroom
> When I was young. Ballooning and mincing airs
> Put on in the 'down there' of England. I was
> Already out of place . . . .

I think of the geographical range of her work as I circle York's walls for the fourth time – on my way to meet her for the first time. I had added fifty minutes to the journey time, for getting lost, and am now late. I park at an expensive hotel, book a table for two for dinner and get a taxi which takes me to our meeting point in three minutes. I instantly recognised the figure I had watched in a dozen or more TV programs about Egypt or archaeology. Seriously attractive with a halo of red hair caught by an autumn sun, outer-framed by the beautiful old King's Manor of the University of York; the first thing that struck me was her spontaneous warmth. The second was how genuinely unaffected Dr Joann Fletcher, Honorary Research Fellow and Consultant

Dr Stephen Buckley and Terry Mullen, Deputy Head of Penistone Grammar School. *The Author*

85

Egyptologist to various museums and media including the BBC is. The rest filters in over time, though I realised quickly that scholastic and bright, she is also feisty, innovative, determined, articulate and tenacious enough to disprove the stereotypical disbarment of gender.

It is my first visit to the university and I am happily surprised to meet her colleagues before we go off to talk. The one I recognise instantly is Dr Stephen Buckley. A forensic archaeologist his particular interest is the unique embalming techniques of the ancient Egyptians and their sophisticated use of tree resins and oils to kill the bacteria which would have decomposed the bodies. He was with her when the monumental and televised discovery was made in tomb KV 35 in the Valley of the Kings. They dovetail and match to perfection; he reserved and with an automatically analytical mind, and she vivacious and laterally intuitive, sharing the same fervent intent. It isn't about proving that they are right in their identification of the three bodies; it is more about inspiring others to care who and what they actually were.

According to her mum, she first announced that she was going to be an Egyptologist, when she first saw the pictures of the discovery of Tutankhamen's tomb. It took a little longer for the incongruity of a little girl in a Barnsley school with such an ambition to convince anyone else; but then, archaeology is a slow business. She was six or even younger at the time. Being part of a family which has, and shares a love of history, fed her growing interest. An aunt, who had herself as a child been inspired by stories of the 1920s discovery of the most lavish tomb in history, added to it firing her imagination with 'colourful tales' and memories. Whilst others of her age were besotted by the Osmonds or David Essex, for Joann Fletcher it was a nine year old boy pharaoh. In 1972 the unprecedented splendour of the treasures of the Tutankhamen exhibition hit London on its world tour, and every school in the country 'did' its own version of Egyptian history. A new sister, born the same year, kept budding expert Joann Fletcher at home however, to begin what would become a lifelong collection of information and memorabilia.

Publications of the day indicated our still naive knowledge of a culture, a dynasty and an era. It is quite remarkable when compared with the wealth and fascinating depth of information in Joann Fletcher's *The Search for Nefertiti* which followed some thirty years later. On reading her account for the first time I had the feeling that I was meeting real families; discovering all that there was to know about them and their lives. Reaching back four thousand years into every undetected nook and uncontrived cranny, it is a real reality show; people and the way they went about living their daily lives eating, drinking, working, sleeping, learning, dressing up, following fashion trends, playing games, choosing toys or jewellery, their interests, skills, buildings, culture, dynasties, beliefs, traditions, sex lives, quarrels, medicines every aspect of their way of life – and their way of death. It becomes utterly fascinating.

The first steps in that journey came when Joann Fletcher was fifteen. Opposing certain archaic attitudes towards teaching methods in her high school for girls' education, she recalls constant failure to persuade teachers that her interest was either realistic or relevant. She recalls being set one piece of work, to find information on two gods from other religions. She chose Horus and Isis. 'No, no, no, I said gods; they are not gods,' came the ill-informed response from her teacher as an assessment. The effect was a complete turn off. She recalls a reduction of motivation in other subject areas too, as they all increasingly became relatively unimportant and totally uninspiring. 'History and Latin are what you will need to do,' was the careers advice she was eventually given. 'But I knew already that was not specialised enough; I saw it as proof of their disinterest in my ambition, but got on with the work.' She studied alone much of the time, reading for pleasure anything she could her hands on about the past that was to become her future.

Wisely, her parents, who had originally thought 'she would grow out of it,' now accepted the inevitable, and let her go on holiday with the aunt who had started it all. It was a 'dream come true' holiday for them both; for one a present to herself on her retirement, for the other the start of a dream which would come true. The decision was bold; Egypt was in a state of turmoil only days before the trip was due to begin, following the assassination of its President Anwar Sadat. One of those most mysteriously magnetic places which most people plan to visit at some point in their lives, the pyramid skyline image of Giza or the sight of the Nile by moonlight is stunning by any standard. Anciently wonderful and so long dreamed of, the most recognised place on earth viewed from the air was 'incalculably mind-blowing' leaving her sleepless with excitement.

'The tour' was typical, a superficially swift program of laid out days to do what tourists do, glimpsed views and statistics of Cairo's mosques, tombs, museums, pyramids with a dusk finale of 'a cheesy yet strangely wonderful' 'Sound and Light' show. From Giza to Sakkara to Luxor 'that once was Thebes,' knowing what footsteps they were walking in left her astonished, inspired and with a now insatiable appetite to want to know everything there was to know about the place. A last day return to the museum in Cairo probably set her course for life. It is a prerequisite for being an adolescent; to challenge, to question, to debunk or simply to reject the accepted. Consumed by curiosity, she took notes amassing a list of questions which seemed to challenge the very foundations of versions given or books she had already read. 'Why did Ra and Horus look the same?' 'Why did Isis wear Hathor's head-dress?' The guides were pleasant, but with acceptable answers being less forth-coming a personal lifetime quest began. She felt she had to resolve some of the mysteries surrounding the lives and deaths of not only Tutankhamen, but also the exquisite Nefertiti and her husband, Ahkenaten.

There seemed little prospect of that on a return to school and a set of O level examinations which she regarded increasingly as unrelated to her unswerving intention to study for a degree, in Egyptology of course. She would have to go London, and opted for University College London; as geographically close to the British Museum as she could get. It also had the first Egyptology department in the country, having been set up in 1892 – as the result of the efforts of another woman. In preference to Oxbridge colleges Amelia Ann Blandford Edwards chose University College for her bequest as the only one which admitted men and women on equal terms regardless of their religious beliefs. Giving up on further efforts to gain support outside the family, Joann Fletcher had chosen 'A' levels to support her aim, wisely it seems as, aged eighteen, she was given one of the few places UCL offered each year. Here her voracious appetite was fed by the quality of the tutorship, reading Edwards' own books, and meeting research fellows who had actually studied with Margaret Murray, Britain's first professional female Egyptologist. I can hear her impact on the young Fletcher as she recounts a Murray BBC interview, 'I heard this amazing academic saying, I'm a piece of archaeology myself, being ninety-six!' I take to the woman myself on hearing her auto-biography was entitled, *My First Hundred Years*. You'd have to have her as one of your 'ideal guests round a dinner table' wouldn't you?

The other person Joann Fletcher met during her time at UCL and to whom gives recognition for her kindness, support and advice was another woman, Julia Samson. Her knowledge of the Amarna period, and her publications which contradicted established views fired the student's imagination lighting a flame which is carried through her own search for Nefertiti. It also helped her to understand, though never accept, the origins of the perennial insistence that the field of archae-ology is a male province. 'We have to bear in mind that these women were absolute groundbreakers, working in a man's world in an age when women who only wanted to vote were being imprisoned.'

What she didn't realise then was she had become something of a role model herself. One of her younger sister's school friends was closely watching ' . . . her progress, vitality – and all that hair' says another like-minded Titian haired individual. 'I was drawn by the sheer enthusiasm she had for her subject she was then and still is my inspiration and

Dr Joann Fletcher. *The Author*

definitely my working role model', says Dr Vanessa Corby who now digs equally deeply in her own field of study – the effects of working class input on the arts. Her definition of the arts includes ethnicity, gender, sexuality and geographical implications exposing truths that are at best regrettable and at worst shameful. For years this young academic has researched and voiced a clear and present warning which government ignores at society's peril.

'If the present levels of government funding and student debt continue a crisis in the arts is imminent. The voices of a younger generation of the working classes that would speak of their experience in Britain via art, film and literature are in danger of being silenced as their opportunities are denied'. Following her role model's lead she questions recent government statistics on working class students' applications 'which claim numbers are as good if not better, post tuition fees'. Her own experience in two universities over the past twelve months however indicates 'reductions by 17% and 23%' and what the figures don't look at is the knock on effect for postgraduate recruitment.' She is validating the gut instinct views I hear expressed in schools every day as wise and experienced middle managers question a policy which actually funds the closure of successful arts courses and with them nurseries from which their successors would come. Weep and howl again.

It is strong but clear stuff, and over eighteen months after first hearing her speak on the subject I find myself in February 2007 hearing different versions of it on every newscast in the day as minority youth seems to short circuit by opting for unacceptable alternative routes to 'power'. Refusing to engage in dialogue only at the level of the already educated or to be confined to the bulging shelves of academia she has a plan currently on hold as she puts all her efforts in to a new post at the University of York. At some point following the publication of her second book, she will take her work to the road with a mystery play style format in the hope of engaging a new listener; the general public. Exhibitions in and out of traditional gallery space, screenings, readable pamphlets, catalogues, audio and visual guided workshops and even a television programme aimed to appeal to and to involve those very audiences who express feelings of exclusion to the very edges of our society. Called *Common Sense* it is a foxy twenty first century artistic production of theatre, cinema and literature which cocks a snook at out-dated notions of current class differences. Spotting her mischievousness, I check the Oxford English reference dictionary for alternative uses of the common word. Firstly it is: occurring often; then: shared by or coming from one source; before it becomes: low class, vulgar or inferior. It is common sense really isn't it?

It is also an open invitation to a different party, which allows anyone to join forces with artists, playwrights, scholars and critics in recognising the quality and the potential of the arts in cultural development for the well-being of our society. Music to my ears, her tune is one I wish Alec Clegg and Michael Sadler could listen to, and I'd gamble that David, Richard and John Attenborough, Andrew, John and Peter Clegg will. I just have this faint concern that Davies Giddy on the other hand could be thinking,' What did I tell you!'

Joann Fletcher who virtually made her own educational opportunities left UCL in 1987 with an Honours degree which predictably included hieroglyphics to which she then added a Certificate in Entomological Studies at Cambridge, a PhD at the University of Manchester (Ancient Egyptian Hair: a study in style, form and function) and finally a University of Cambridge Certificate in Arabic and Arab Studies in 1996. A reasonable scholastic performance one might think, but not enough to stampede dinosaurs. Some of her 'old deficiencies" were ingrained it appeared, and the dour predictions of unsuitability went on. Grudging acknowledgement of the quality of her results might offset the fact that she had spent more time in Manchester than Cambridge; but she also still dressed exactly as she wished. Even when told, 'There is a sort of academic dress code, you know . . .' she opted for large silver and semi-precious stoned jewellery worn on understated long sartorial lines, always in black and doing for the cluttered look of the 1980s what Beau Brummell did for the fop. 'That was how I wanted to be, looking at the window displays in Pollyanna every single day as I went home from school.' Like her role model, Rita Britton, in turn she too deliberately kept her accent, flatly refusing to soften the vowels of her beloved home county. But worse still, daring dreams in what remained in male territory, she was still female. So she is; but not much given to taking up the female prerogative of changing her mind – or her style. So it seemed that if the 'modern' pundits were correct, she was never going to make it in her chosen field. And strangest of all, the place where she was accepted with trust and respect was Egypt itself. She sat at the feet of the people who knew most; those whose gift it is to see below the surface and beyond appearances, and soaked it all up.

Despite the prophesies of home failure from abroad, from 1990 to 1995 her rapidly energetic and expanding contribution impacted on a published range as comprehensive as the *New Scientist*, research at the University of Leiden in Holland, *Time Life*, the British Museum and the Hairdressers' Journal International. I ask her about the Tutankhamun Wardrobe Seminar at Leiden University in Holland, and she grins on learning that Joan Booth attended the same school as she did, and is now is its Professor of Classics; the first woman or English person in history to hold that position. Realising that Joan Booth is the acknowledged expert on Ovid's poetry she takes details to contact her, 'Fantastic; I never knew she was from Barnsley – the Ovid links are crucial!'

Fletcher's own expertise was increasingly being sought in the growing media and public interest shown in ancient hairstyles (three generations of them in her family, don't forget) as well as wigs, cosmetics, perfumes, body oils, tattoos, jewellery. Multiple TV channels satisfied historical and geographical appetite and she became the ancient world's new wonder; an expert on fashionable styles and beauty products, but from four thousand years earlier. It is now unthinkable that any media archaeological coverage of that field would not consult her.

Her humour draws me; skittish, self deprecating, skimming at the same time as being seriously clever. She has the capacity to catch the eye and engage the mind of readers of *The Sun* and *The Spectator*, with the same headline. Since he first heard her lecture in those indifferent days of 1995, she has had the same effect on one of the world's leading authorities, an archaeologist who does accept and seems to admire her protestant style and catholic impact. Professor Earl L Ertman's early support and faith in her future has been a confidence factor without which she may have faltered, and which she will never forget. It is, I suspect the reason for her totally positive support and personal encouragement for every student or child's interest in Egyptology, whether that be concrete-set as her own was, or a fickle and fleeting interest. Combined with the specific focus of her thesis and her personality, it is easy to see with hindsight what has made her the force to be reckoned with that she undoubtedly is today. There is a fine line between passion and obsession which Joann Fletcher knows well, and she is passionate, now in her quest to put the past into every child's future. In 2003 she made a little history of her own by designing the first GCSE-equivalent (Level 2) qualification in Egyptology. As I watch her inspiring youngsters to dare to dream their own dreams at school Speech Days, it is interesting to watch shrewd headteachers, staff, governors and even pupils moving in to pick up on it, and on her.

Her Wakefield Museum lecture in 2006 attracted just such proactive managers of high quality educational opportunities, and she was persuaded to agree to do inputs at both Penistone Grammar School and Wakefield Girls High School before she left. Since she is in negotiations with influential film producers for the filming rights of her published work on both Nefertiti and Cleopatra it is entirely predictable that there

Joann Fletcher with Wakefield Girls' High School student, Lara Wild – also applying for a university place to follow Dr Fletcher's lead. *The Author*

will be a surge of interest in Egyptian influenced clothing, hair make-up and perfume. 2006 saw the University of York introduce her first Egyptian archaeology module into its undergraduate archaeology degree course; which she now teaches there. The world and the odds have changed; and the smart academic money it now seems, is on girls doing both archaeology and Egyptology.

Her tenacity has proved her right in that but also in her long-held assertion of the significance of Yorkshire in the history of Egyptology. There had been pilgrimages to the Holy Land for centuries which eventually included a detour visit to Egypt, to what they believed at the time to be granaries, the great storage places of Joseph's biblical corn in Egypt. As long ago as 1610 it was one of the first of these tourists Yorkshireman George Sandys who, realising that they were actually the tombs of kings, wrote the first English account ever to say so. An acquaintance of Bram Stoker, Durham ex-miner Sir George Elliot, presented an Egyptian mummy to Whitby Museum after, it is thought, Stoker had been inspired to write *The Jewel of Seven Stars* with a mummy as the main character, on a holiday there.

I'm fairly pleased with those snippets, but ready to cheer when the next bit of trivia is forthcoming. When Howard Carter, of Tutankhamun fame, left the employment of Theodore Davies, an American who funded many excavations in the early 20th century, to work instead for Lord Carnarvon, his place as official artist was taken by a man named Harold Jones. 'Jones, despite always being described as a Welshman, was in fact born in Barnsley where his father was head of the local art school' Joann Fletcher informs me with equal parochial pride. You won't find a member of the Fletcher family with a bad word to say about 'good Yorkshire folk'. They are steeped in the history of the place, the people and the traditions. Guides to the city of York, her parents refute the bad press given by Shakespeare to Richard lll; a much maligned lad in our shared view. That's not to say we find all Yorkshire folk blameless, only most; though some, like Robert Holgate, may have been a bit misguided.

Ostensibly, Henry Vlll's visit to Yorkshire in 1541 was to enable any complaints of injustice against his Council of the North to be made formally to him. Despite the fact that bills of complaint poured in, after examination by the King and his Council, unsurprisingly every single one was declared false and untrue. The President of that Council, Hemsworth born Robert Holgate, was also appointed as one of the justices who found Catherine Howard, Henry's fifth wife and Queen, guilty of 'acts of infidelity' whilst staying at Pontefract Castle. Her execution following a trial at Doncaster was in turn followed (coincidentally no doubt) by Holgate being made Archbishop of York.

Terry Mullen and Jane Liddy, Head of Wakefield Girls' High, Pat Langham with Jo Fletcher and Stephen Buckley. *The Author*

As such, Holgate was the first bishop to take the new oath acknowledging the King's supremacy and renouncing the Pope. His loyalty to the Crown was clear again as he immediately transferred to the King the ownership of forty manors in Yorkshire, with others in Nottingham Northumberland, and Gloucestershire. He does seem to have amassed great personal wealth whilst being accused of impoverishing the See of York in his support of the King. But times change and dangerous times even more perilously; after the death of Henry followed by his son the young Edward Vl, Holgate faced the Catholic Queen Mary Tudor. His houses, goods, plates and jewels were seized in 1553 and he was confined to the Tower for 'divers offences'. He survived but eventually died back at Hemsworth, regarded poorly as having 'brought about a great scandal and disgrace'.

Not without the occasional breath of scandal himself, Henry Vlll's reputation fared rather better, due largely to his administrative adroitness and innovative ideas. With no standing army to protect against invasion, his policy of creating Lords Lieutenancies across the nation was financially as well as politically astute. By choosing men who could both raise an army and contribute to its upkeep, in case of invasion by the Spanish Armada, the country's defences were strengthened, and those taking the role had enhanced standing. 'The status of the role has varied; strongly supported by Elizabeth l, there were wholesale changes during the reigns of James ll and Charles ll, and again through industrialisation, ' says David Moody, Her Majesty's Lord-Lieutenant for South Yorkshire since 2004. 'Today's Lord-Lieutenants are selected for different reasons and with very different roles. Now the Prime Minister advised by the Appointments Secretary, in turn makes recommendations to the Queen.' 'So who advises the Appointments Secretary?' I find myself asking.

David Moody, the modern holder of the ancient title tells me, 'There is detailed inspection of the credentials of prospective holders of the office. They have generally featured in public life and been recognised as acceptable for their contributions in other appointments, such as High Sheriff of the County, Deputy Lord Lieutenant or Master Cutler.' He, I note, has two out of three of those qualifications, and more. 'As they will be expected to be in office for ten years or more, age is a factor; as is health due to the large number of engagements undertaken, which also means that not being involved full time in a career is a consideration.' I suspect the old banking reference requirement will also apply; respectable and trustworthy. 'The PM's Appointments Secretary visits the area with a fine toothcomb, identifying what is expected to fulfil the duties of the role and then takes suggestions from a wide range of sources. A list of appropriate candidates is drawn up and fine-tuned and the appointment is made under Letters Patent.'

It's that archaic language that snaps the mind back into focus; this isn't just a job for anyone, it is for the personal representative of the monarch in a specific geographical area. Inspection of troops is part of that role, and presentation of degrees, awards and honours, if received in the home county rather than at Buckingham Palace and being patron of a range of non-political organisations. Historically aristocratic, it is now increasingly the peak of industrial, professional or commercial recognition. If that suggests pomp and ceremony, the booted and spurred regalia can take up to half an hour to put on. But you meet the man, not the uniform, and informality, genuine interest and friendliness are his dress code. 'For me the basics of the job comprise firstly, the Royal ceremony and welcoming them to the county, or representing Her Majesty; citizenship ceremonies which are new, and the law which is historic. Then there are educational contacts with schools, colleges and universities; and military links with regiments and veterans as well as the

The Lord-Lieutenant of South Yorkshire with the Bishop of Pontefract.
The Author

voluntary sector and community awards, and the regeneration of South Yorkshire.'

David Moody's first job as a graduate apprentice in the steel industry might not be seen as an obvious choice for an MA in Modern History from Pembroke College Oxford. What it did give him was wide knowledge of a massive private industry becoming nationalised, industrial relations and all that was entailed in that, as well as the marketing of the company to add to his production experience. Additional study at the London Business School combined with carefully planned management promotion back in the private sector, led to him leading the company in the steel industry's first management buy out. Rounded by further experience in property and technology, he was then able to become involved in other areas which interested him. Becoming President of the Sheffield Chamber of Commerce gave him a voice to campaign for the improvement of the Parkway approach to the city from the Ml motorway, so beginning a programme of retaining the best, and replacing the worst with the best. Sheffield is increasingly an attractive city with a treasured past and an equally promising future.

He was also building a reputation as a mover and shaker in the regeneration of South Yorkshire. As Chairman of the South Yorkshire

Investment Fund he was heavily involved in the allocation of funding to regenerate the areas affected by 'the economic problems of the 1980s and 1990s'. He now looks back on that as one of the 'buzz aspects of the job'. He does enjoy the opportunities he now has to meet the 'Royals' and especially the Queen, who he describes as 'a charming, remarkable woman, very well informed and one who has earned the affection and genuine respect of the country,' and clearly his too. As a history buff, modern and ancient, he looks at how the monarchy has evolved and dealt with change during her reign. He doesn't believe in change for change's sake; arguing for reform or improvement with reference to how things are. It's music to my ears and I wish he'd chosen education as a career. But when I ask what the biggest thrill of this unique office has been, it is not privileges of that order; it is that he has 'been given the opportunity to play a small part in the remarkable revival that is happening in South Yorkshire.' I begin to see what that fine tooth comb would have rooted out.

The origin of his office is evident in links to The Army Benevolent Fund or Royal British Legion, and newer contacts with Community Foundations. But I'm interested to see the reflection of his personal interests in the surprising range of other involvements the office has. His own love of classical music is shared as Patron of 'Lost Chord' providing high quality music to elderly or dementia sufferers. The Doncaster Minster Appeal, Friends of Sheffield Cathedral and Yorkshire Historic Churches Trusts are a pleasure to the man whose interest in visiting churches he describes as 'a passion which has taken me world-wide.' Not least is his other passion which is to contribute further to the regeneration of the former coalfields' communities by means of education and the provision of facilities such as through his involvement with the National Coal Mining Museum.

I suspect he is reticent, wary of appearing too proud of himself rather than of the honour he attributes to the office itself. Clearly a man who learns from every experience, he brings a wealth of it with him to a post he sees as needing awareness of the past whilst looking to the future. He acknowledges the weight of the office as heavy with history, but lightens it with a great, almost impish, sense of humour. His biggest concerns on any official visit are his wish that it should be informal; and his hope that he won't fall over his sword. Falling and swords come to my mind since just across the valley he lives in, is Wentworth Castle, once the home of the 2nd Earl of Strafford. After a meteoric career leading to him being closest adviser to Charles 1 and made Lord-Deputy of Ireland, the first Earl of Strafford fell from grace after refusing to support the levying of taxes for an army against Scotland. The short and the long of it, in parliamentary terms, was his impeachment. He defended himself so well

The Mayor of Barnsley, the Lord Lieutenant of South Yorkshire laid the first wreaths at the first Memorial Service to be held to remember those who died as a result of working in the coal industry. The service was conducted by the Bishop of Wakefield and the Rector of St Mary's Church Barnsley, the Rev Ian Wildey. *Photograph by kind permission of Brian Elliott*

The altar of St Mary's Church – Miners' Memorial Service 2006. *The Author*

The families of miners leaving St Mary's church after the service. *Photograph by kind permission of Brian Elliott*

that it was impossible to find him guilty, and a Bill of Attainder was obtained and used by parliament enabling him to be found guilty without the trouble of guilt being proven. 'That was a very early example of retrospective legislation,' he comments wryly, 'we are getting more used to it these days!' When he was beheaded on Tower Hill in 1641, Thomas Wentworth had been Lord Lieutenant of Yorkshire from 1628. But as David Moody says, if you are aware of the past you are less likely to make the same mistakes!

So Wentworth's good works are oft interred with his bones; like Robert Holgate's whose are largely forgotten, except in certain free schools. From as early as 1546 he had founded and liberally endowed schools in York, Malton, and in Hemsworth (which endowment was subsequently transferred to Barnsley). Holgate School survives there to the time of writing with some of the town's finest products having been taught there. By the 1950s the addition of an intake of working class potential contributed to an outpouring of athletic and academic achievement which would have put it at the top of any league table. Until quite recently it retained a touching tradition of 'calling the names'. Once a year the names of 'old boys, fallen in the wars' would be called out along its corridors stairways as if they were still there, recalling their place in the school, as well as ensuring their service to their country was remembered with respect.

That's a bit less permanent than the Egyptians' way of ensuring that their ancestors were safely kept, but no less caring than the way Joann Fletcher and Stephen Buckley work. It is a respect that borders on reverence they show as they inspect and decipher, uncover and reveal the fragility of their finds. The build up and then moment they finally gain permission and entrance to KV 35 and first see the three mummies lying there is thrilling. 'It's you!' is her audible response in instant recognition of who the three bodies could be. And her excitement is totally infectious, 'I never ever thought I'd see that day! It was very emotional, wonderful and terrifying, at the same time, but in one sense the fact that the TV cameras were there helped me to stay calm and focussed.'

Exactly one hundred years after Harold Jones' part in this classic timeless saga, Joann Fletcher dusts off the story with some startling finishing touches. We become a part of it and want those three figures to be 'them' and it seems they are, until we realise that crucially- there's an arm missing. It has been ripped off the body. Then she finds it, but the Professor says it isn't the right one, it doesn't fit. The dust thickens over the plot again, more confusion and questions and the puzzle looks set to stay for decades more, and then . . . Well you really have to read the book.

12

Derek Robinson

'There is nothing in Derek Robinson's kindly academic demeanour to suggest he is the son of a miner.' So began one of the more balanced or less tendentious newspaper reports in the media frenzy which followed the fall of Edward Heath's government. I find this passing introduction to the then Deputy Chairman of the Pay Board staggeringly stereotypical. But then, I would, as would anyone who had met this miner, his father. The writer clearly had not.

Too young to be cannon fodder and not placed to receive an education that would maximise his true potential, Benny Robinson was a well-respected, courteous, honest, trustworthy, reflective, intelligent and also kindly miner. Tall and straight in every sense, he loved the unrestricted freedom of walking in beautiful countryside when he was not underground, and would walk as many miles above ground at weekends as he had crawled in a week's work down a mine. He could tell you the name of every wild flower and tree, where the best blackberries were, exactly where and when cowslips, catkins, pussy willow, and bulrushes would be at their best, and he knew where skylarks built their nests. He dressed immaculately and had beautifully shaped hands and nails, blue- scarred but perfectly kept. A gentle man with a heart of gold which, like his choked lungs and cartilage bereft knees was terminally damaged by working for 49 years in an industry he felt he was pressed into by circumstance, and hesitated insecurely to leave by choice.

Making one bold dash for freedom just before the Second World War, with his young family he moved briefly to Halifax. With the outbreak of war he attempted unsuccessfully to enlist in each of the three armed services. Like so many others he was refused because he had been in mining, and was conscripted back into the coalmines to contribute to the war effort. An effort and contribution that went seemingly unrecognised for decades, until thanks to the wise efforts of a few, miners were given the privilege of marching alongside the armed forces as a part of the nation's Remembrance Day Services. Lord Mason of Barnsley has expressed the view that ' . . . the fact of the matter was that those who knew what life in the pits was like preferred the prospect of going into battle against a deadly enemy'. He would know having begun work at the age of fourteen in a coal mine himself. Admiral of the Fleet Lord Lewin's ADC though later a naval captain, had in fact been a Bevin Boy himself so Lewin was aware of a little known fact. After the war when seeking jobs or places in further education, each of the so-called Bevin Boys had to fight his own battle for recognition of his status as an ex National Service conscript. The two worked tirelessly to redress what they regarded as a national failure to recognise the industry's contribution to the war effort. On November 6th 1998, more than fifty years after the war had ended they were able to announce in a letter to *The Times* newspaper that permission had been granted:

Sir

For the first time in 50 years a contingent of Bevin Boys will march past the Cenotaph after Sunday's Service of Remembrance, bringing up the rear of the procession and recognisable by their miners' helmets.

This occasion marks a milestone in history. The presence of a few survivors of the 21,000 men who were conscripted under the National Service Acts to work underground instead of wearing Service uniform is long overdue. However it is welcome recognition by the Government of their contribution to the war effort.

They were not conscientious objectors. On their call-up they were given no option; even prior membership of the Cadet Forces in the hope of being directed to the Service of their choice was disregarded. The chance of the figure at the end of their call-up number directed them to the mines. The nearest they got to a uniform was the miner's helmet and safety lamp and they were denied the protection of a buttonhole badge, which identified members of the Merchant Navy. After the war each had to fight his own battle for recognition of his status as an ex-National Service conscript when seeking jobs or a place in further education. Mr Churchill recognised their worth and said (Report April 22nd 1943):

. . . one will say 'I was a fighter pilot'; another will say 'I was in the Submarine Service'; another 'I marched with the Eighth Army': a fourth will say 'None of you could have lived without the convoys and the Merchant seamen' and you in your turn will say with equal pride and with equal right 'We cut the coal.'

They certainly made their contribution, even if it earned them neither a demob suit nor a medal.

Yours sincerely

Mason of Barnsley

Lewin

House of Lords.

Tony Benn and Rodney Bickerstaffe with Benny Robinson's great grandson Benny Watson. *Peter Watson*

I assume that his well-fought war will now be over. Not so; having won the battle, he tells me that this war goes on until authorisation to wear their own special badge with that quote from Churchill on it, 'We cut the coal' is given. 'Then I shall be content,' says the ex-miner who has additionally contributed over fifty years of unbroken service to his country in the Houses of Commons and Lords.

Benny Robinson had taken his children, then his grandchildren to stand opposite the Town Hall every Sunday closest to November 11th, removed his best trilby hat and silently taught them the meaning of respect, remembrance, tradition and duty. Sadly he, like thousands of others died before 1998 so never knew the outcome. Born in 1910 he was but one, not untypical, of that wasted generation of bright, un-tutored men and women who had been thrown, before the era of education for life, aged thirteen, into a world that meant work for life. He had a sensitive, enquiring, bright and ranging mind which freed him from a potentially tedious life in the company of Hemingway, Dickens, Steinbeck, Poe, Shaw, Chandler, Joyce, Conan Doyle and Zane Grey. Unlike his wife who although well spoken and clearly intelligent, never stretched her potential beyond reading 'East Lynne' at least once a year plus all the latest magazines. He was a wide voracious reader who loved to browse through the public library, passing on his love and respect for the written word to his children. If his shift work prevented him from doing it himself, the task of collecting new or returning read library books was delegated to them, and he would tut tut and shake his head at the one who missed a new 'good un' or brought back one he had already read.

Benny Robinson's grandchildren and great grandchildren at the 2006 play off – living in Bedford, Sutton Coldfield and St Albans but all still proud Barnsley supporters.
The Author

Youth League Champions 1926; front row centre Freddy Robinson to his left, Benny Robinson.
The Author

In his youth he was a gifted footballer, coached by his father Thomas Robinson, who was trainer of Redfearns Glassworks Football Club when it proudly won the local Junior League and Cup in 1910–11. The glassblower father had five sons who became miners, typifying Barnsley in an age when it was as famous for glass as it was for coal. The town's crest evidences this still, having two supporting figures, a glassblower and a miner, on either side of the coat of arms. These were heady years when football was to the working class what Rugby was to education. Memories of triumph in the season of 1911–12 when Barnsley 'won the Cup' and brought it back to Oakwell were still fresh and conceivably re-enactable. Benny and his brother Freddy Robinson were skilled and enthusiastic footballers who were scouted by leading teams of the day, Birmingham, Leeds and Huddersfield. Following a successful trial, Benny Robinson may well have played for Birmingham, had not a wet-booted, hard-studded, deliberately foul tackle finished both his footballing days and his dream.

These were the days still when youngsters, as young as twelve or thirteen, would have to leave their homes to find the means of making a living, wherever it could be found. Millwork for girls was as common as the rapidly expanding coal industry, but not so much in Barnsley as in the woollen towns. When her father was killed in a mining accident, one such girl, May Blackburn, moved to the Halifax area and found lodgings with a family in Salterhebble. The father was a self-employed painter and decorator, and the mother who could neither read nor write, but was regarded as a seriously reliable worker at a wool mill in West Vale. This was an ethic she instilled in her three daughters, Lizzie, Annie and Gertie, who worked alongside their mother. Their work record enabled them to get their young lodger a job at the same mill, so allowing the girl to earn enough to help support and provide a living for her widowed mother and family. The twelve hour a day week ended, she would travel back home with her wage, often accompanied by the youngest of the three sisters from Salterhebble. They would spend the Saturday afternoon roaming the vast site and grand sight that was then Barnsley market. Saturday night meant deciding which of the local dance halls to visit to be a part of the fast growing and trendy Saturday night fever of the late 1920s and early 1930s.

Following the success of the Charleston, the tango and foxtrot were the latest rage, and it was the local dance halls of the day that were the meeting places for young people. It was at one of these Saturday night dances that the young visitor, Gertrude Mary from Halifax, first met Benjamin Robinson of Barnsley. Both excellent dancers, and snappy dressers, they quickly paired up, danced all night and arranged to meet again on the next Saturday night. For him, his suggestion that they should meet under the clock at Harral's meant he would be on Eldon Street, by a large, impressive clock outside Benj. Harral's jewellers and watchmakers. For her, a comparative stranger to the town, Harrals meant a shop in Sheffield Road that she had seen on the way to the Blackburn house. Both turned up on time, both waited and then both left. Luckily they both chose the same dance hall to go to the following week, and so met again. After a year or so of bus and train journeys back and forth between the two home towns they married and settled in Barnsley where he could find work.

As was the custom, young expectant mothers would go home to be with their own mother for a home confinement, so just before the birth of their expected twins, Benny Robinson's wife went back to Salterhebble. In the worst winter in living memory, with no doctor present, the twin boys were born, one of them survived the other did not. Benny Robinson registered the death of his stillborn son and, in drifts of snow four feet deep the child was laid to rest in a shared grave of one hundred stillborn babies in Stonygate graveyard, Halifax. The same day he returned to work in Barnsley followed, after her recovery, by his wife and surviving baby son, Derek. Proud and devoted, they watched carefully as he grew and developed as part of the close-knit extended family typical in mining communities. Tom Robinson and his wife Mary Ellen's house was in turn first home to each of the brothers when they first married, three of whom, Charlie, Freddie and Benny then moved into neighbouring houses in the same street. The remaining two, Eric and Ken, also lived close by.

From the start Derek Robinson was a bright and able child, who also played and enjoyed sports. He played football, and rugby both at school and for the Barnsley Youth Team, and flirted briefly with an amateur dramatic group, with people who went on to make it a part of their lives; local drama mentor Felix Squires, and one Stanley

Mary and Benny Robinson with their young son Derek. *The Robinson family collection*

Richardson, better known as Stan Richards or better still as Seth from *Emmerdale*. Robinson dropped the dramatics but retained the stage presence, along with other memories of growing up in a mining community that remain clear, perceptive and powerful.

Some pits were reputedly militant, deemed always ready to strike unofficially. His father was not a militant man in any sense, but like virtually all the rest would not, could not, blackleg. Memories of coal-picking and hungry families in the 1920s were still raw, leaving many resentful or angry, but also worried. Traditional values of loyalty and workmate solidarity were inbuilt and instinctively unbreakable. If there had been a dispute which remained unsettled the next shift would not work. It was a long walk or the wasted cost of a bus fare in these days, when word of mouth was the only source of information for these families. Children would run the errand to find out from workmates on the previous shift if the next shift would be working or if the dispute was unresolved. Derek Robinson recalls the many times as a lad he would be sent running from one end of the town to the other, to check if it was worth the journey for his dad to turn up at the pit and be able to work or not.

It was fortunate for Benny Robinson and his brothers that they did not work the shift at Carlton Pit on August 6th 1936. All fifty seven miners who did were killed in an underground explosion and one more died later. National Union of Mineworkers archivist, Phil Thompson, informs me that the number of fatalities was seriously reduced because Barnsley FC was playing an important home match. Benny Robinson who should have worked, but was due to play football himself that day, swapped his shift. The workers who arrived at the pit head after the disaster were given the task of going underground to recover the bodies of men they knew and worked with. For some that meant friends, for some relatives, and for some men they had swapped shifts with.

They collected limbs which they carefully tried to piece together to look like whole corpses, blanket-covered over to conceal the war-like remains. Then they stretchered them past sobbing but otherwise silently waiting women at the entrance to the pit. In the sleepless nights that renewed that horror periodically throughout his life, Benny Robinson could never forget and never forgave that experience. For that day's work of getting, not coal, just flesh and blood, they received no pay. So 'No lad of mine is going down t' pit,' increasingly became the mantra of the generation.

To ensure a safe grounding for educational success even before the 1944 Education Act it was necessary for children to have access to 'a good school.' That, for the Robinsons, meant that their son needed and won, a County Minor Scholarship in order to gain admission to the town's Holgate Grammar School. Clearly an able all rounder, keenly interested in learning from an early age, he performed well in the school which would subsequently earn the derision of a contemporary, Michael Parkinson, or being part of a town which 'did for education what Myxomatosis did for the rabbit.' A view not shared by another contemporary, the late but much loved in Barnsley still, Brian Glover. Up to his death, this internationally renowned and regarded actor regularly visited and supported any project linked to the town and is fondly remembered for his loyalty, as he countered with his view that the school had 'done alright by him!'

Robinson recalls now that acceptance for the privilege of entry to the school entailed his father having to agree that his son would remain there until the age of sixteen, taking the School Certificate public examination. Any early leavers' parents would be required to repay the costs. So despite completing his School Certificate exams at fifteen Robinson remained, taking the national civil service examination. On the day he became sixteen he left and took a job as a temporary clerk in the town's Inland Revenue offices.

The civil service qualification, and a widely held view of his general ability and aptitude, led very soon to him being appointed to a higher grade and transfer in the block recruitment of able civil servants to staff the administration of the newly formed Ministry of Health on the introduction of the National Health Service in 1948. He would live in London and work at Whitehall; so despite his youth his parents supported the move to what they regarded as the ultimate success. This naïve, low-esteemed unawareness of the full range of entitlement, opportunity, aspiration and potential is in evidence still in youngsters in many working class areas today, despite half a century of legislative and educational attempts to overcome it.

Crossing the north south divide in 1948 was even more of a leap than it is today and a sharp learning curve, Robinson wryly remembers one decision taken in his first days in Whitehall. He was assessed as fully competent to undertake all aspects of the work, but with one exception. He should not answer the telephone. His northern accent rendered him totally unintelligible he was told. This would be in pretty much the same way that the BBC immortalised Halifax's Wilfred Pickles, in deeming him unsuitable to read national newscasts, one assumes. Looking for people who spoke the same language irrespective of their vowels, the young civil servant joined the South Kensington Labour Party, became an active member of the Civil Service Clerical Association, and also played rugby for Osterley. Within two years he was conscripted for National Service, which he served largely in Kenya, and there played for the East African Command Rugby Team.

On completion of his National Service he returned to London working in the Ministry of Health and playing rugby for Mill Hill, until an injury forced him to give it up and move back to football. Living in Stanmore he now joined Harrow East Labour Party, where he was befriended by one, Merlin Rees, who on his way home would give the youngster lifts back to the hostel where he lived for the next two years. He became a CSCA conference delegate and attended Union Summer School and Labour Party Schools, becoming increasingly active in both trade union and Labour Party matters. He was also given advice by Rees, that he should extend his educational experience in order to reinforce sound opinions of his own. Increasingly certain that the advice was equally sound, he returned to Barnsley. There he worked in the National Assistance Board at Wath on Dearne by day, studied for 'A' levels in evening classes, and played rugby again for Barnsley.

It was whilst in this post that portents of his future, as a peerless authority on pay structures, might have been spotted. At the 1955 annual conference of the Civil Service Staff Association he proposed a motion to change the system of remuneration based on age increments, which he and other young employees regarded as unfair. Waving his own pay packet in the air, he joked that he, and any fellow employee, would be fifty-three years old before they could achieve maximum pay. He reportedly received an enthusiastic response from the floor, and from the press, but the motion was not carried. It was an early recognition of perspectives, anomalies, relativities and straightforward perceptions of fairness. These, ironically, together with Robinson's future suggested policies on wage structures, would one day become universally accepted by scores of governments world wide. But at this stage it merely re-enforced his view that he felt he was being fobbed off with economics and needed to learn more.

So he applied for and was awarded a TUC scholarship to study for a Diploma in Economics and Political Science at Ruskin College, Oxford, where he met and relished the new company of seriously interesting and stimulating people, including Jean Lynch, a like-minded, positive and bright fellow student. She, although being from Ilford, seems to have had no problem, in understanding him despite the accent when he proposed to her. She accepted and they set up home in Oxford as he applied for and won, one of thirty Mature State Scholarships that were then available to enable more mature students access to a university education. With that and her support and with an inherited work ethic for which he is still admired; he was able to undertake a full time degree course, gaining a first in Philosophy Politics and Economics in just two years.

Briefly leaving Oxford for a spell at the Extramural Department of the University of Sheffield he became involved in teaching mainly trade union classes, largely derbyshire miners, on a scheme of higher education jointly arranged by the NUM and the NCB. In 1961 a research post on wages arose at the Institute of Economics and Statistics as Assistant Research Officer which drew them back to Oxford. Subsequently promoted to Senior Research Officer, a post he retained until retirement. In those early days he, with Sid Kessler the Research Officer of the National Union of Mineworkers held the first ever national summer school for the NUM in Oxford, on the future of the coal industry. One of the students on the first week was Mick McGahey, who would later become Vice President of the National Union of Mineworkers.

Evidencing a rare ability to teach the full spectrum of ability, he additionally held a post as part-time lecturer at Balliol College, and by 1969 had declined a Chair at a prestigious northern university to accept a Fellowship at Magdalen College, where he taught Economics until

2006, long after formal retirement. Those who know these things will tell you that there is no better place in the world to read Politics, Philosophy and Economics than Magdalen College Oxford. Those who have done that will speak in the same terms of Derek Robinson. So may those at the Universities of Berkeley, Cornell, Hawaii and other seats of learning where he has undertaken visiting professorships.

Like any other, the day job of an Oxford don brings its own demands and rewards. For Robinson the demands fell well within his capability enabling additional extensive research work. Increasingly he was, and remains, recognised as reliable, thorough and skilled in his chosen field, spurning the notion that he is objective by questioning what objectivity is, when I suggest it might also be a factor. Invited to become Economic Adviser to the emergent National Board for Prices and Incomes, his input from 1965 to 1967 further improved his national and international standing. Strongly recommended by officials there, in 1968 his family read press reports of him being flown back from teaching at Berkeley, California to be offered the job as Senior Economic Adviser to the newly formed Department for Employment and Productivity by Barbara Castle. 'There is a limited field to choose from, of which he is the best,' was the advice given and taken. Gregarious, empathic and witty, he was also regarded as a practical, universally aware, trade union-savvy academic, with more knowledge in the field of wages than anyone.' He was thirty six years old.

This was what he identifies as the biggest challenge he had met so far in terms of both demand and influence. Now he would be involved in Cabinet sub-committee groups advising at the highest level with acute awareness of the impact that could have. Throughout these years his stock remained as high as his profile was low, as he continued to teach,

Derek Robinson and the Secretary of State for Education, Shirley Williams. *Derek Robinson's collection*

to research and to publish. Never forgetting his own roots and routes he continued to contribute to seminars and summer schools for TUC representatives, working with and enjoying friendships with names now famous in trade unionism, including Len Murray, Rodney Bickerstaffe and Norman Willis who had also been a contemporary at Ruskin College and university. Robinson's views were universally respected and sought on all aspects from wage drift and structures, manpower distribution, incomes policies, capital sharing, negotiated savings plans for workers and countless others.

By 1973 a different government under Edward Heath recognised that there remained a growing sense of injustice following the pay freeze it had introduced in 1971, due in part to anomalies created by it. Why wouldn't there be? The past three decades of improved educational opportunity was creating a new class. It was not the riotous sedition that Davies Giddy predicted, more an articulate and informed wind of change blowing fiercely through tradition with views of hard work deserving fair play and fair pay. To report publicly on these anomalies, thereby hoping to dampen the growing flames and upheaval of industrial unrest, the Heath government set up a Pay Board. Its brief was to report on the treatment of anomalies; other difficulties of pay relativities and finally to recommend how these issues could be addressed. Successful outcomes would of course contribute to the effort to control inflation. Time was of the essence in staunching the increasing loss of worked hours and days through industrial action, and dates were set for its conclusions to be made public. The NUM had a serious wage claim and after an overtime ban, had called a strike. The country was on a three-day week.

Robinson's long held view that fairness, like beauty, was in the eye of the beholder was increasingly to become recognised as pivotal in terms of negotiation and settlement in those dispute riven days. As possibly was his sage awareness that 'it is the fish that chooses the bait, not the fisherman.' Certainly Prime Minister Heath knew well his pedigree, his reputation and his achievements when appointing Derek Robinson as Deputy Chairman of the Pay Board. His listings in *Who's Who* and *Debretts* had been clear enough for long enough that no-one need not know. A great irony is that President of the National Union of Mineworkers, Arthur Scargill, also from Barnsley, did not know who he was. Until the die was cast the following year, he had no idea that the man who had heard the miners' case was from his own home town, and was part of a family that he did know. Robinson knew the anglers, the fish and the range of baits available.

I ask Derek Robinson why he thinks he was given the task of preparing the report on fair distribution of wages, or relativities. He is

The Pay Board: Miners' leaders Laurence Daly, Joe Gormley and Mick McGahey. Deputy Chairman Derek Robinson is 4th from the right on the 2nd row. *Derek Robinson's collection*

perfectly clear in his view, and answers in the same moderate and modest mode his father would have. 'They put me on because of my knowledge and experience in that field. They wanted an academic; they knew I was pro trade union and that I had at times been critical of Labour. They also, knew by the way, that my dad was a miner, and that he was on strike.' He goes on to add, that he didn't realise at the time that the majority of members of the Pay Board who were as stringently vetted as he had been, turned out to have links to the mining industry ranging from vet treatment for pit ponies to running personnel policies for NCB white collar workers.

The Board's findings concluded that if a group of workers had been paid unfairly compared to other groups, it should be made a special case. The NUM executive had stepped up their action in recommending a strike by a majority vote of 16 – 10. It would have been possible at that point for that strike to be averted had Willie Whitelaw taken the 'special case' stance. He chose not to, later admitting however he had not thought through the implications of it. Heath, at the time and for some years, blamed Robinson in particular for what he saw as contributing to his defeat at the general election that he had called.

Robinson, professionally affronted at the time is now phlegmatic about what he describes as an example of 'the cock-up rather than the conspiracy theory.' The fact is that he had personally checked every single figure in the pay Board's investigation. The cock-up was that civil servants working on the government's figures had not, and they were inaccurate. The problem was that the NCB in calculating average earnings for miners did so in a way that was different from the way in which average earnings for all other workers were calculated, with the result that miners' wages appeared higher than if they had been calculated in the same way as all the others. This made it appear that miners were relatively better paid than they were. An important part of the miners' claim was that they should be top of the earnings league, so the different method of calculation had significant misleading effects. Not one Conservative Minister who could confirm their figures or supply further information was available in London at the moment that it became crucial for the Heath government. Wilson was triumphant about the figures confusion, Heath went to the country, and lost the election.

Years later, at an Anglo American conference at Ditchley House, Heath and Robinson met for the first time. In the lounge of the beautiful old former home of the Wills tobacco family, the bow-tied television journalist Robin Day, chatting to Robinson, pointed out that Edward Heath had entered the room asked if he had spoken to him. 'Never met him,' replied Robinson, giving no indication of any desire to do so. Day then approached Heath who presumably gave a similar response commenting that he was tired, and soon afterwards left the room. 'Some time later he returned,' Robinson recalls, commenting that the former Prime Minister had obviously at least begun to prepare to go to bed, 'he came back with no tie and his shirt neck undone, and walked straight across to where I was still sitting.' Day introduced them and Heath's first words were, 'If it were not for you, I would still be Prime Minister!' Robinson's reply was equally direct, 'That is yet another mistake you've made Mr Heath!'

Heath asked what he meant, and Robinson pointed out that his view was that Heath had made two major errors. He had called an election on 'Who governs the country?' and then announced that he would accept the recommendations of the Pay Board. 'Doesn't that rather imply that the Pay Board governed the country?' he asked the former PM. 'And the second?' was Heath's only reply. 'Statistics don't bring down governments. Misuse of them does,' said Robinson pointing out that after finding a typing error in the Pay Board's documentation, he had personally gone through the entire report checking every single statistic himself. The result was that at no time did any official suggest the Pay Board's calculations were inaccurate. 'You relied on civil

Derek Robinson presented to His Majesty the King of Spain. *Derek Robinson's collection*

servants who did not do their homework properly – their figures were wrong.' Heath's response to this was another question, this time rhetorical and amazing. 'Why didn't anyone tell me that?' The two then talked for hours on what was or wasn't, who did or didn't and may be what might and might not have been.

As is often the case, it's the newsworthy item, exchange or involvement which makes the headlines that stay in the mind. Good news is no news. Robinson's work since then has been no less influential or impressive in terms of output and quality; it has been simply acknowledged or reported in a less sensational manner. Following the Pay Board, he was appointed Chairman of the Social Science Research Council leading to recognition in the New Years Honours List of 1979, awarding him the rank of CBE. During his three years there he chaired an enquiry into the system of remuneration of members of local authorities. He was also appointed to the British Library Board, which doubtless would have pleased his dad. Much later he would work as Inter-regional adviser to the International Labour Organisation which included two years in Geneva, with countless other intercontinental consultancies taking him from one end of the earth to the other.

His publications are seminal in both international policy frame-works, and the teaching of economics. As recently as 2006 Emeritus Fellow and Lecturer in Economics and also academic supervisor in charge of visiting students from America, he was lecturing to the Stanford University campus at Oxford, retaining still the highest esteem as befits such 'a very experienced scholar'. Largely based in the room he occupied for nearly half a century with views of deer roaming beautiful grounds, his familiar figure is instantly and affectionately recognised, and was so long before and since his term of office as Vice President of Magdalen College. 'Oh Derek? He's not arrived yet but he's due, he'll come flying round that corner any minute,' I was once assured by a Gate Porter when I arrived early for an appointment, and on the hour he did. He is a rarity too in that he loves his work and has often commented on what he regards as his good fortune, 'I've got a job that's better than working. If I wasn't a trade unionist I would do it for nothing!'

There are no differences in his response whether to kings and heads of state or working men. The common touch that helped make him remains intact. Knowing the heights he scaled and the weight of some of his offices I am often asked if it has changed him. The answer is I

Derek Robinson and Nelson Mandela. *Derek Robinson's collection*

think not. Recently, artist Ashley Jackson, when appointed a Freeman of the City of London, spoke of other people the system of honours has or has not ever fully recognised. He asked if I knew about Derek Robinson, the Oxford don and world famous economist. When I replied that I had known him all my life, he asked why the man had not been included in *All for Barnsley*. As Jackson pointed out, 'He's probably the biggest international heavyweight the town has ever produced!' I could only reply, 'I know, Ashley, but he ain't heavy.'

13

Tracy Wilkinson

Drew Barrymore is really cool. Or so I am reliably informed by Mimi and India, my grandchildren who know these things. She was, in any event, looking cool on the front cover of *Entertainment*, displayed on every news stand in every drugstore in California, the week I arrived in Los Angeles. She was wearing a T-shirt designed by the woman I was there to meet, fashion designer Tracy Wilkinson. A 'bird from Barnsley' now living and working in Los Angeles, Tracy Wilkinson had from an early age shown inclinations towards both migration and fashion. It was most likely she thinks, the long summer family holidays in France in her childhood that started it. For her friend of those days, Joanne Short, those coastliner memories of blackberry, chocolate and wine-sensed days gave the taste of the novels for which she now receives world-wide acclaim as Joanne Harris. For Tracy the fascination was the casual and carefree style she saw in the local fashion.

Back in England, Wakefield Girls' High had and retains an excellent record of great academic provision and achievement. It was however, less well resourced and diverse in its focus and provision for the Arts; as this perceptive young student readily identified. With the support of the staff in that area she began a pragmatic campaign to have Fashion and Textile Design introduced to the curriculum. Responding positively to the initiative and accepting the criticism as constructive, management approval was given – along with two sewing machines. It was through this good result that Tracy Wilkinson realised with reason and effort it is possible to obtain backing and practical resources, for what hopes and dreams alone will never provide.

Her designing days really began to take shape at that stage as she admired the sweetness and simplicity of the summer clothes she saw worn by young girls in France, and felt the influence leading her already into what was to become her own signature style. Careers advice that she should not chance the risky fashion business, but take journalism as a career option, she instantly discounted, knowing already what her mind was set on. She applauds the wisdom of her parents at that stage, in realising that this was no whim, and that she had the capacity to finish what she started, and that she would do her best in her chosen field. 'They're not gamblers by nature,' she says of her accountant father and mother, who is the daughter of an accountant, 'but they were prepared to back my instinct.' She then adds her view, that it was Dick and Bernice Wilkinson's 'annual audit' of her performance and examination results which ensured that their financial backing was less at risk. It was that too which made her feel she had to 'stick at it.' It is with immense affection that she recalls that early evidence of trust and faith in her ability, and commends it as sound parental practice.

Looking back she recalls herself, naïve and relatively innocent, and finding the move to De Montford University, Leicester exhilarating. She loved the freedom, challenge and upbeat pace of the artistic and intellectual rigour. She felt like a sponge soaking up everything, and suddenly thinking that anything was possible. 'It was my first taste of real independence and I was absorbed by an amazing burst of the release of creativity. I could create all day long, and for the first time I felt what came out of me was almost uncontrollable, it was initially quite scary, but then exhilarating.'

I believe that each one of has in our memory a special, ideal age which is fixed in the happiest, nearest to ideal years we can remember. It is our age at that time in our lives which, given back our yesterdays, we would always choose to be. For me, it began in my late thirties and lasted throughout my forties, for her it began then and could be anywhere from the age of eighteen to thirty. It was at this point that she first felt that the bird was symbolic of her philosophy, with its connotations of peace, freedom, independence, simplicity, sweetness and happiness, and its ability to fly high.

Armed with her first degree she was accepted three years later by the Royal College of Art in London where she took the opportunity to develop further her abilities and strengths. When she left in 1988 it was with a Masters Degree in Fashion Design to take to New York where her first experience with Banana Republic demanded producing as many as one hundred and fifty knitwear designs each season, and presenting them coast to coast in the USA, Italy, Hong Kong and the UK. She hopped from one branch of the business to another, constantly learning the rudiments of the industry. Confident enough by this time, she moved into freelance designing which gave her more freedom, and choice in what she could select and reject. She trade marked the brand by which she is now known internationally – Mon Petit Oiseau, and within a year her little bird was included as a logo on every one of her garments.

Two years later she was on the move again, this time to Los Angeles, where she was contracted to Mossimo as Design Director of the women's division. She regards this as a steep learning curve experience, as looking around she saw herself as part of a team of young and talented people, but who were increasingly designing what they were told to design. 'What that company was clearly good at was hiring self-starters,'

Mimi Watson wearing 'the T-Shirt' with a mini skirt bearing the Mon Petit Oiseau motif. *The Author*

she tells me, 'since twenty per cent of those kids who were in that team are doing well in their own businesses now, in PR, in Design, in Graphics and in the creative field. Then we were not satisfying our true creative abilities or even developing them, and you have to believe in your ability to do that because ultimately that is what you will stand or fall on.' The company was making big money, but she was unfulfilled, so confident that she had done the spadework, mastered the skills she would need she set up again as a free lance.

The start was tough she recalls and for the first two years she couldn't pay herself a proper wage, and was working harder than she had ever done.

It did not affect her determination however, and having rejected a work style that told designers what to design, and then blamed them if it didn't sell, she was ready to stand or fall on her own judgement and merit. She had, she is quick to point out, that one additional asset, strongly supportive parents who still believed in her judgement.

'I really don't believe that everyone has an equal chance in life, it is not fair, but it is a fact. For some their early life damages them too much, so it drives them out of the system. For others a similar experience drives them to prove that they are somebody or can be something.' I understand what she is saying about those who lack the ability, will, drive or stamina to take what the world throws at them, 'We all have to learn the lesson and develop our own strategies for ourselves.' Looking as if she is still in her twenties, but too sage by far to be it, she fields the view that 'the middle of the road is very often for the middle classes. Hollywood is the classic 'It might happen' world, based more on dreams than on means, but you really do have to be realistic. Americans expect the American Dream, which is why there is the level of credit and debit debt there is in the USA. My peers here find me comparatively negative in investment, but I'm just cautious being from a working class background.'

As one of my eyebrows half raises a query she quickly adds, 'Being brought up in a family of accountants in a working town like Barnsley ensures caution and that you keep your feet on the ground wherever you are.' In any case it is who you are and what you think you are that really matters. Like Vanessa Corby, she maintains a positive position on 'working class' which working for oneself doesn't alter. She is fully prepared to take the risks that have to be taken and balanced against potential success, and then to live with the outcome. For her, that has become part of the buzz, and she rejects working for others as too stultifying.

Interestingly, she has kept the loyalty of her former employer Mossimo as an account, as she had Guess, and her growing reputation which eventually brought her accounts like Puma West and DKNY. Her biggest early break, she feels, came when the tall, slim, stylish and still girl-like designer was spotted wearing one of the T-shirts she had designed, by a buyer from Fred Segal who promptly asked her to design a whole range for them. Following the excellent reception to the ensuing range, she realised that she could again do for herself what she could do for others and went completely solo from design to manufacturing to sales.

She had experienced over the years virtually every aspect of the industry, from fabrics to design, from production to sampling, from management to finance, in fact all that is required to succeed in business after a great deal of really trying. The sheer relief of the move, and the sense of independence and freedom, brought back the memories of her earliest and her happiest days. She was struck by similarities between France and Los Angeles, in the climates, warm and sunny, and the informal life styles, cool but chic. That, she decided, would be her direction; pretty and delicate, soft and simple tops and trousers, skirts and dresses, and a range of lingerie. Her target would be to reflect the choices of still made by women in their early twenties, whilst simultaneously appealing to the notoriously difficult and fickle teenage market.

The potential was tremendous, the concept rare, and if successful seemed to offer the elusive, if not almost impossible answer to a riddle as old as the sphinx. How does a mother let a teenager choose for herself what she wants to wear, and finish by paying for exactly what she would have chosen for her too?

The independence came at a high cost, but she prepared herself to work night and day, and would do any job that the business required of her in those early days. Her designs were not cheap, but had the quality and style to warrant the price. 'No-one can please everybody, so I don't even try.' She knows enough not to be hurt if a buyer, after viewing the range, says 'I don't like it .' She always made a point of listening to find out why, philosophically pointing out that they would sometimes have a very good idea that was worth taking on board. She would then' tweak a little', adding or removing some aspect or other, or changing the colour.

If, however, she has 'the right feel' about a range, she will stick to her guns and let the public decide. She has great respect for her longstanding customers, and will sell direct to them to reward them for their loyalty.

Tracy Wilkinson at work in LA.
The Author

A sneak preview of the season's range. *The Author*

That represents not only a slow and steady build up of clientele, I realise, as I meet some of them in her showroom. It is much smarter than that, she has an automatic feedback service, straight from the hip market research direct feedback. They chat as they look through the range, fingering the fabrics, holding up garments, as they tell her where they have also seen them on sale, would normally shop, where they go to wear them, who else has them, how they feel as well as the kind of comment or response they have had, when wearing their last purchases.

She has an enviable and influential range of A List clients too. Following her magazine cover appearance the week I was there, Drew Barrymore personally requested the same garment in every other colour. Her taste is shared by Reece Witherspoon, Mary Louise Parker, Rose McGowan and Christine Ricci. They are all equally cool my teen intelligence agency assures me. As I wonder if she feels she has reached a comfortable stage where she can now relax, she starts to enthuse about her new range and slight shift in direction. Still happy with her stock-in-trade junior look, which she knows will be in demand while ever the young care about their carefree appearance, she points out a more sophisticated edge in some of her Autumn range. She identifies it as 'vintage years' which to her are the 1960s and 1970s. She recalls the hours she spent scouring Charity shops as a very young girl, looking for the just gone out of fashion bargains. 'I loved that, personalising, re-shaping, re-styling and customising those gorgeous fabrics into my own styles.'

I too can see the nostalgia in her sharper, slicker, into a business edge that these new garments show, and recognise myself as having loved and worn clothes reminiscent of, but not the same as them, from

Copenhagen to London. They were the days of a fashion revolution, the time that Rita Britton, 'an absolute marketing genius,' developed the unique Pollyanna in Barnsley, she reminds me. She adds herself to list of admires of individuality of that order, but has no designing icons. She does admire the Italian Marni line, Marc Jacobs and Chloe, but draws a finer line between the flattery of imitation and the theft of plagiarism. 'To be influenced by a recognisable talent is one thing, but then to try to sell it as your own creation is quite another.' She is in a position to know that, having to apply for Cease and Desist Orders on an almost weekly basis to prevent her designs being flagrantly copied. 'It stops that single offence, but you have to be philosophical or you'd spend your entire life trying to prevent it and that will never happen, it's worldwide.' She then goes on to name one company which systematically buys her garments and manufactures cheap copies of them in Hong Kong.

She wouldn't ever think of Hong Kong as a base for her own company,

Yorkshire Fashion Idol 2006 winner young designer Lisa Mitchell, maybe hoping for advice from established international designer Diane Bates, before launching her first collecting in 2007. Diane Bates' own ongoing 'Painted Lady Collection' comprises the beautiful masterpieces that she describes as 'a Hybrid' art anchored in aspects of embroidery, fashion, sculpture and fairy tales.' It is quite simply, exquisitely wearable art. *The Author*

and particularly not now as she sees Los Angeles emerging strongly as a fashion manufacturing centre. Through its network of contacts and an increasingly large immigrant population she sees it eventually being in a position to replace Paris, which has held on to its place largely through its early tradition of designing talent, she feels. New York could be a possibility for her in the future, or maybe even London, but her favourite re-location would be Palm Springs.

So where is she going, if as she says, she can't stop yet, because she hasn't finished? The waking dream for her goes on and now includes a plan to create a multi-national brand. With local partner interest and potential, brokers, lawyers and investment bankers already in the frame, she is looking to a market as diverse as Japan, Korea and Europe. The requisite thirty million pound entrance figure doesn't even raise a blink, as she raps out range expansion, hosiery, swim wear, children's wear, department stores, wholesalers, sales representatives, and the eventual exit strategy. Political correctness, it seems, has not yet reached all the United States, as she takes a firm stance on the still evident male domination of her industry.

She is totally unhindered by her tall, blonde, willowy appearance in their macho world, and will not accept being downgraded as just another minority group member. In a recent meeting one of her ideas was peremptorily dismissed by one male dinosaur saying, 'You talk just like my wife.' Laughter ceased and a frisson ran through the room as she faced him squarely and asked, 'Is there a man in this room you would have said that to?' She rolls out an impressive CV if needed telling them, 'I'm not just a blonde who designs clothes!' Even her language is tuned to the assertive American style of 'this will happen' and not 'I hope to'. It retains its English quality, but just like her standards meets them halfway across the pond. The accent isn't the basis of US snobbery, but snobbery exists just the same. She earns the respect she gets, walking the talk, rapping out the jargon, knowing the business and not suffering fools gladly. 'Women have to be tough to make it here; it's not enough to show assertiveness, you have to show you can do the job.'

The woman who did her own deliveries driving a pick-up truck around the USA in the tough early days will not now defer to the macho -suited men of the West, it is plain to see. She is set on making it even further, delivering her business plan as well as the goods. The little bird, it seems to me, is flying high enough to be easily taken for an eagle.

14

Stephen Moody

I've always been star-struck! I think it comes from spending half your childhood in cinemas, blazing away at Saturday morning singing-alongs as one of the boys and girls well-known as Minors of the ABC, before racing off to the pick of the afternoon matinees. It was a fibre rich diet of Roy Rogers, Gene Autrey, Laurel and Hardy, Superman, Flash Gordon, The Three Stooges or The Last of the Mohicans. In school holidays or when he was working night shifts, my father would collect me from school and take me with him to see the latest released film noire at the local cinema. Humphrey Bogart was his favourite, so *To Have and Have Not*, *Key Largo*, *San Quentin*, *The Maltese Falcon* and the like, became the unlikely, early favourites of mine too. Protected by him, but also by a censorship system, I would sit happily unperturbed watching films then rated as adult viewing, and grew to recognise stars like George Raft in *Shanghai*, Kirk Douglas in *Champion*, and John Wayne or Errol Flynn winning wars across the world and the centuries. I would watch the news too, Movietone or Pathe Pictorial, with occasional items from Hollywood where stars hand and footprints were set in concrete immortality outside Graumanns' Chinese Theatre, and dream of being there one day, but never really believing I would make it.

But it is a beautiful California day as my hostess in Hollywood, Mary Valentine, drives us along the coast at Malibu. I've wanted to be here too ever since I first saw it through the eyes of Sheilah Graham, 'wickedly' living with Scott Fitzgerald in a house they called 'Honi soit qui Malibu.' Finally I'm here where film and political intrigue and history are lived out still on a beach lapped by the Pacific Ocean. There remains the distinct possibility that you could turn around and find yourself recognising the familiar face of someone you had never actually met. Not today though, it's blue-rinsed, pooch-petting owners, and braced-toothed, forced-laughter quad bikers only, not a star to be struck by in sight.

I have to settle for concrete unreality outside Graumanns, along with the constant stream of others drawn by fairy tale dreams or warm memories. I'm surprised by an inexplicably strong sense of attachment though, and find it's enough, to think that you are standing in the footprints of the great and the gone. I take the mandatory snapshot for my grandson, Benny, who has spent hours with me watching videos of virtually every musical ever made old and new. Having just seen *Grease*, his current hero is John Travolta, and there they are, his footprints near to my own unsung all-time hero, Donald O'Connor. He is the man, probably best remembered for his song and dance routine including a run up a wall and back-flip back down in *Singing in the Rain*. How different it might have been for him, and for Sean Connery, if O'Connor had accepted the role for which (not a lot of people know) he was Cubby Broccoli's first choice – to play James Bond.

The building on Santa Monica Boulevard is impressive, with a balcony from which you can the Pacific Ocean. They are very proud of their building and designing prowess over there, so I am reluctant to point out that Benjamin Latrobe, who set up public architecture in the United States, was actually born in Pudsey. He not only designed the White House porticos and St John's Church I was shown in Washington, but also the Basilica of the National Shrine of the Assumption of the Blessed Virgin Mary in Baltimore – America's first Catholic Cathedral; the Pope House in Lexington, Kentucky; the Taft Museum of Art building in Cincinnati; as well as the oldest building in continuous use for medical education in the entire northern hemisphere – the Davidge Hall at the University of Maryland. Oh, and the United States Capitol building in Washington, DC!

In this particular 146,000 square feet of 'prime realty' I am sitting on the second floor waiting to see the man described as 'one of the most inspiring artists the beauty industry has known,' the International Executive Director of Education of the Vidal Sassoon empire. He has, just the day before, returned from Japan, and is leaving again the following day, this time for South America, but has found time to see me. His diary for the day is packed and at least a dozen people have shot in and out of his office in the five minutes I have been sitting there. I am already feeling slightly nervous about meeting him, and as I am handed a copy of his CV to read as I wait, I note that he began in 1990 as a Vardera. I am now in big trouble before I even get in to meet him, realising I have no idea what a Vardera is.

Before I can think of a subtle way to find out, a smiling Cyndi Wakita tells me, 'Stephen will see you now,' and shows me into his office. As I enter the room he is speaking on the telephone, but smiles beckoning to me to sit down, indicating that he is ending the call. Smiling back I look round the room, thinking I might spot a labelled photo of a Vardera, which could give me a clue to what one did, but if there is I can't see it. There is however, on the wall above his desk, a great picture of him with Vidal Sassoon, and it instantly occurs to me how similar the two are in appearance, and I note, they both have a great head of hair. He is dark, handsome and articulate giving the immediate impression of being both

Stephen Moody.
The Author

capable and amenable. Almost at once he replaces the handset and stands up to shake my hand, and I note he is also tall! 'Barnsley eh? It's good to see you.' I feel at once that it is going to be alright, and we might not even get round to Varderas, as he says 'It's always good to hear a Yorkshire voice.' We are up and away, instantly swapping stories of accents versus dialects, mispronunciations and people we both know, as we discover yet again, that the world is only as big as a small former mining town in Yorkshire.

So far as he is able he hangs on to his own accent, though travel has routinely polished it to ease and ensure global comprehension. He mentions a British TV crew filming out there some years earlier, doing a series on Yorkshire ex pats. 'The bloke presenting that series was brilliant, and whilst stubbornly proud of his own strong Yorkshire accent, he was incredibly expert on others. Big, bearded and wearing jeans and a checked shirt, he came across initially as 'blue collar', and because of that people here initially made the mistaken assumption that he was not well-educated or widely read.' The former Vardera took his visitor to the local British pub where the Yorkshire man overheard two girls talking at the next table. Assuming it would be Yorkshire pub protocol as well as grub, the newcomer asked them if they were from Carolina, but got the Santa Monica response of a silent reaction to strangers. Undeterred he commented that is was clear that they were anyway, and it was South and not North Carolina, then closed his participation by pinning it down to less than fifty miles from where the girls were born! 'They couldn't work out how he done it, and thought he must have asked someone who knew them.' Stephen Moody is still obviously tickled by both the incident and the northern Henry Higgins' ability to carry it off.

It wasn't just the visitor's ear that was keen it seems, Moody describes him as having eyes like a hawk too, not missing a thing and even spotting a book entitled, *The Bus to Barnsley Market*, on a shelf, when filming at the Moody's home in Malibu. On being asked if he had read it, with a grin, Yorkshire TV presenter Ian Clayton replied, 'I wrote most of it!' He did too, the book was edited by him, Brian Lewis, then of Yorkshire Arts Circus, and me in the late 1980s. Based on the ways of life and education in Barnsley and the surrounding villages, from the 1930s to the 1980s, it included many stories from the community in which Stephen Moody was born and bred, and had to leave behind in the move to California. 'My mother gave me three bits of home to bring with me when I left England. A piece of coal I still keep to remind me of the industry that my family came from, a silver tankard to remind me that Barnsley Bitter was the best in the world, and this book so I never forget who I am, and my American born children would know where our roots are.'

'Walking down Santa Monica Boulevard with Ian Clayton was just like going back home to Darfield, you know how everyone speaks to

Ian Clayton.
The Author

everyone. He stopped every ten yards or so, pointing things out, asking questions or just saying hello to complete strangers as we passed, full of interest, enthusiasm and this amazing fund of knowledge.' I know the feeling, having had similar experiences with him in Barnsley, Pontefract, and all over the county. People are infected by his big grin, ease of manner and instant engagement. He is the walking epitome of mining men that were, but are no more. Once met, he easily dispels the un-informed notion that even some viewers may have originally had, that he is a manufactured Yorkshireman. He is in fact just himself as he ever was, and you can tell instantly that he has been the same all his life, wiser than his years, and that as a child he would have been colloquially referred to as 'old-fashioned' by fond adults.

I have only known the consistently great Ian Clayton since he was about twenty years old, but will wager that he has been just the same since he was three. His latest book, *Bringing it All Back*, does just what it says on the cover. It is about his life and loves; his family, music, history and people. So many of the memories that he has in his amazing head at any one time are blissfully recounted through music and his love of it on a journey through his life from Batley to Baton Rouge, Dodworth to Dallas, Kinsley to Karachi, Mapplewell to Memphis, Tadcaster to Tennessee, Wombwell to Witicha and then to Hay-on-Wye, which became a personal Hell. It ends as does everything I have ever known him say or do, with a dream, a hope, a shaft of sunlit promise or the optimism of his own, very individual faith. To have your heart lifted and broken and lifted again in one small volume – read it.

He is just the kind of bloke too that Stephen Moody misses in being away from home, along with his family and one or two other things. 'It's mostly the humour, there's nothing quite like it. I miss the put downs, the slow timing, the self-deprecation and reality of the humour that they don't seem to do here, American humour is so totally different.' We're off again, swapping memories and jokes, and put downs from stand-ups, professionals in Working Men's Clubs to gifted amateurs in the work place, comics all. I had, just before leaving for the US, been to the funeral of one of the all time best of the professionals, dear, dear Stan Richards, better known as Seth of Emmerdale. News of his death had not yet reached Los Angeles, due in part perhaps to the marked reluc-tance of the company to write him out of the script, of the currently highest rated soap in the UK, despite his long and life-threatening illness. Momentarily he is saddened by the news of the death, but then I tell him how virtually the entire cast and company of the award-winning show had packed into the little church of St Thomas, Gawber, to celebrate the life of the nationally respected local hero.

There were great and funny loving tributes by Richard Thorpe aka

Alan Turner, the only longer serving member of the cast than Stan, and Chris Chittell who abandoned Eric Pollard's insincerity. Then Stan's son Allan gave a star performance in delivering the eulogy on behalf of the family. Born to make people laugh, was how Stan Richards had always thought of himself, from his early days as a Melody Maniac, through all the wry and comic performances that marked his seriously successful acting career. He was incapable of taking life or himself seriously, even ironically, when the family sat at his bedside through the night on one of the three occasions they were called to be there for the last rites. One of the nurses, called in to say she was going off duty for a few days, an ominous sign for the family who realised why she had come to say goodbye to their father. With a last look at the comatose patient she said she had to go as she had a pile of ironing waiting for her at home.

They all turned in total disbelief as his eyes flickered open and Stan's voice asked 'Have you heard the one about he woman who was ironing her bra when her husband asked why she was bothering when she had nowt to put in it.' Their grins got even bigger as he managed the punch line, 'I know, but I've just ironed your underpants.' Stan Richards on his back, but back on stage, back in business and ready to laugh and fight on for another eighteen months before finally taking his last bow, but not before he was feted by the Emmerdale company after receiving a standing ovation at the BAFTA Awards. It will be another six months after my visit to Los Angeles before Seth is actually laid to rest in a story-line that runs for a whole week and actors long gone from the series return to pay tribute to both the man and the character.

So how do you get from there to this very different world he lives in here, I wonder? 'Well my mum was a hairdresser,' he tells me, as if anyone who had lived in Barnsley wouldn't know about Denise of Darfield. She had bucked the traditionalist trend, from shampoo and set to wash and go, as early as the late 1960s, storming a small local business into a Sassoon style salon virtually overnight. You could get a razor cut for one shilling and sixpence in 1968, and Denise Moody could do two of them amongst up to ten roller sets in an hour. She wanted to train to be one of the first of the Sassoon stylists in the north of England. It was an enormous gamble, but she took it. Using the money she had been saving for a new automatic washing machine and borrowing the rest from her father, she closed her salon for a whole week and invested everything in enrolment at the London training school. She accepted the philosophy and mastered the techniques, including the trademark Five Point cut. Vidal Sassoon himself rated her as 'a dedicated student, high praise, and given only when it was well earned. On hearing that she intended to set up with his revolutionary styling in a small village near Barnsley, he warned her that it was too risky a venture. His own well-researched expansion plan included opening in King Street, Manchester, but not for another five years. 'He was unsure the north was ready for him,' she tells me, 'I was certain it was.'

Denise Moody arrived back home, both qualified and quaking. At this early stage the precision cut could take from two to three hours, which would take the old shampoo and set system out of the equation. She was convinced once local people saw the dramatic styling it would take off, but had no idea how to get things moving quickly. The brainwave came, and she visited every boutique and store in the town giving out fifty vouchers for free haircuts. The condition was that they had to be redeemed by the following week, which turned into the worst waiting week of her life. She had no take-ups until the very last afternoon, when a young woman a with waist-length hair arrived with a voucher, asking if it mattered that the voucher wasn't hers but had changed hands six times before she got it. It didn't, and Denise of Darfield was instantly up and away as a clean cut classic Sassoon stylist, whilst sub-letting salon space to others for the more traditional work.

Her son's earliest memories include living in that house where she first

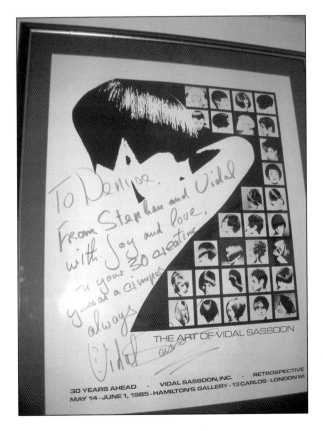

THE ART OF VIDAL SASSOON

30 YEARS AHEAD · VIDAL SASSOON, INC. · RETROSPECTIVE
MAY 14 · JUNE 1, 1985 · HAMILTON'S GALLERY · 13 CARLOS · LONDON W1

Congratulations from Vidal Sassoon and Stephen Moody to Denise Moody. *Denise Moody's Collection*

132

began her career, 'I was actually born in a bedroom in my parent's first house, over the room where she began hairdressing,' he recalls, 'so the scent and sounds of the business were there for me from day one.' Her success in the business led to the first of a series of moves to bigger properties, up to the point where separate premises became a necessity.

He remembers hours watching fascinated as Denise transformed clients before being old enough to join in tidying trays, sweeping up, and then making the first career move, to Saturday boy. He loved it, and it looked like a foregone conclusion that he would go straight in to the family business. In those Thatcher days he recalls, any job was a job worth having, especially in the pear-shaped world of aspiration and prospects in the coal and steel environment that South Yorkshire had become. Teenage ideas do not always sit easily with working for one's parents, so life, never being that straightforward, led him to a completely opposite direction. He decided to enrol on a course to begin to train as an engineer in the steel industry. His recollection is that he knew the first day that he had made a huge mistake, but with his parents' philosophy of integrity, consistency and staying the course, he completed what he had undertaken. The time was not wasted; he made new friends, learnt new skills, successfully qualified as an apprentice engineer and with top marks on his placement, he won the Student of the Year Award. The following day he quit, and went back to hairdressing.

He applied almost immediately for the Beginners' Course with Vidal Sassoon Salons in London, and was one of four of more than a hundred applicants to win a place. Loving it and soaking up the quality of tuition whilst practising developing skills with a natural flair, he worked as never before. 'It's a genetic thing, this work ethic, not only the culture you're raised in,' he says. His father worked all his life, first as a miner, and to the present day as a hairdresser. His grandfather was a miner, a fitter, who considered himself semi-retired when he cut his working week down to five days. His mother is still a total workaholic who he wishes would now 'step off the gas a little.' He repeats wisdom he was taught from the earliest age and has never had cause to doubt, that the only place success comes before work is in a dictionary. 'Big rewards in any business mean big efforts have been put in,' he says, and in his specialised line of work it means not only 'grafting' but putting in the travel too. 'Mrs Smith's appointment for the same style every week does not give a wide enough perspective to get to the very top in this job. That is not what education at Sassoon is about.'

He compares it to an origins-rooted mining industry, identifying the trap of being historically tied to the pithead, as much by limited expectations as by the convenience of nearby clustered company housing. We are together in our total agreement that there is no more point in dwelling on lost industries than lost causes, but forgetting ones history is not an option for us either. He targets youngsters who under achieve because they feel they have no alternative than to remain in the poverty or benefit traps of decimated former industrial areas. He is equally saddened by what he regards as a growing trend of instant gratification. 'Rather than working for what they get, even in the very young, there seems to be a perception of entitlement rather than reward for effort.' I'm reminded of his mother's passion for a career that sacrificed a washing machine, resulting in three years of visits to a launderette.

His fervent belief in education as a force for good is for lifelong and varied styles of learning. Whilst acknowledging that university is not the route for everyone, he is animatedly enthusiastic in his desire to fire up the remainder to also consider moving out of their home bases. He believes too that life and travel are great teachers. 'The easiest place to lose your way is in a small town with nowhere to go, just by staying there. Until you take the plunge you have no idea how much you could achieve anywhere else in the world just by taking your home-grown talents with you.' He identifies what he describes as Yorkshire characteristics, with those of the American Mid West, gritty, honest, strong, hard-working and unafraid of challenge or obstacle. 'My parents taught me all about hard graft, keeping my feet on the ground and sound professional skills. Those are skills which are easily transferable; all you have to learn is how to adjust. You need not be tied, either geographically or professionally, and you're not tied to any particular strata of society either, unless you choose to be.'

His brother Chris is one who chose to make his own success by doing the exact opposite. With no reservations about being a member of the family business, his view is that the bigger challenge is staying in the village in which he was born, and being a part of its regeneration. Declining the whole range of wider opportunities available to him by living and working in London or abroad, he is equally successful in his own field. For him it is the mechanics of the business still, creatively styling his own clientele on a daily basis using equipment he has helped to design and develop. The latest technology, used to introduce electric scissors which combine heat sealing of the ends of the hair whilst cutting it, are a part of the work for which his involvement is internationally recognised. He is also Artistic Director for the entire range of Redken products.

Stephen Moody started out in 1980 and within three years had worked his way to become Principal of the London School. Within two years he moved to the internationally renowned Mayfair Academy and just one year after that was offered, and took up the challenge of opening at the new North of England Education Centre in Manchester.

Following these successes he was promoted and became Principal of the North American Academy. 'My own involvement now is education, and I love it.' He finds attitudes to learning differing enormously across the world and relishes the challenge of adapting presentations and programs. When I ask Vidal Sassoon about this meteoric rise he is instantly clear in his judgement and view of the former Vardera. 'Stephen's qualities are vast; he has the talent of a teacher which gives him the ability to inspire his many thousands of students over his prolonged sojourn with us. He also has the talent of a creator and has been a total joy to work with over these many years. He is held in enormous respect by the industry for the gracious manner in which he conducts himself.' What Stephen Moody says of people who have inspired him is that we all need more than one role model because everyone has failings, flaws or some weakness. 'If you select wisely and realistically as well as idealistically you will have enough to widen your scope to be anything you chose. Have your rebellion early then go on for the real things in your life.'

The lad who once thought it a long journey from Darfield to Pope Pius School in Wath, now routinely travels the world. In any year he will work in Japan, Iceland, Australia, Russia, Korea, South Africa, South America and the whole of Europe, and has trained himself to sleep on trains and boats and planes. 'Of course there are downsides, 'I miss Maria, and my three children.' At the age of three Chase, the eldest, would tell everyone that his daddy worked at the airport, the place they so frequently took him and picked him up from. He regards himself as even luckier now than he thought he was when he first met then married Maria. 'She is a great mother and that's apart from I being a talented artist, a wonderful colourist, she also makes an input teaching here at the Academy, and is amazing interior designer,' he is clearly delighted to tell me. That makes them a home-fixing dream team since his way of relaxing from travel is to do the work on home improvements himself. 'Home is more important if work takes you away so much; I love to get back and start on the house, though that's often just when Maria is fit to be tied and wants to set off and go somewhere.' In the current month he has been at home only ten nights, 'Not a life that every wife would or could cope with,' he emphasises, showing me pictures of Maria with Chase and the twins Cora Lyn and Catcher Dennis whose second name is for his Yorkshire great grandfather.

When he asks how Barnsley is going on, I instinctively know he means the Football Club, not the regeneration program. He can close his eyes and still see the crisp green stripes of its turf in winter sunshine low enough to dazzle the goalie at the Kop End in the second half if they lose the toss up. Red shirts, white shorts, mud loaded and studded boots on centre forwards who could wellie a leather ball into the back of the net from the halfway line, so the place erupted onto the legendary Oakwell roar. And the smell of Bovril at half time! 'Do you know,' he smiles 'I can see and hear that place every time I smell Bovril.' That glorious season in 1997 as the Reds delighted the world playing their heroic, but outclassed, way through the Premier League was a journey back home he would have happily made for every match.

He takes every available opportunity to visit his family and old friends, but loves the family to visit Los Angeles too, telling me of the day he took his nephew with him for a ride on his prized Harley Davison. Having been a motor cycle fanatic since childhood, he was thrilled to pull up next to a really great vintage Indian bike. Still ogling the bike, to get a closer look he dismounted as fast as he could before it pulled away, and in doing so kicked a man standing behind him. Apologising profusely he turned to hear a deep guttural voice saying, 'No problem' and found himself looking at a smiling Arnold Schwarzenegger. On a slow news day anything that happens in Malibu is at risk of appearing in the media, so there is an unwritten law that people who live there routinely observe that the A list residents are not approached when going about their private lives. 'He realised that my nephew was a visitor from England and a great fan, so readily signed an autograph for him and really made his day.' Comparing instances of what he has read in the press compared with what he actually knows to be the case, he is

Pub Grub
California style.
The Author

defensive of Hollywood stars and critical of the treatment they some-times receive.

The analogy he draws is untinted in the roots of his personal memories of the UK-wide strikes of the1970s, when he was still at school and the even more memorable year long struggle of the Miners' Strike in 1984. 'That is a classic example of how news can be manipulated to produce the desired effect,' he feels, going on to recall his all-time favourite film, *Brassed Off*. We are in unison in identifying the highs of the film, but also in one criticism. There were no circumstances, however dire, that the Peter Postlethwaite character Danny would have sworn as he did in public at the end of the film. That was 'pit talk' and would never have been used by him in mixed company. He hasn't yet seen the story told as it really was in David Thacker's wonderful 2005 drama for the BBC, *Faith* which featured local actors and characters. He makes me promise to get a copy for him.

His packed schedule means we have run out of time, but he has to eat so suggests we go across the road for English pub grub. I conceal my cynical wariness at the thought of good English pub grub on Santa Monica Boulevard, and am proved right to have done so! The Churchill Arms bristles and buzzes like a real pub and really does serve great bangers and mash; too great to be followed by a pudding. 'No you have to try the rhubarb crumble and custard,' he insists, ordering one portion and three spoons. This is new territory for Hollywood resident Mary Valentine who tells me she had not set out that day expecting to spoon over an English pudding with 'The Stephen Moody.' It's a score for the eccentric English I feel, and then I remember that I still don't know what a Vardera is. And that's when I realise that it no longer matters to me, and that it never did to him anyway.

(A Vardera is one who is prepared to work for no pay initially in order to gain experience and to learn the rudiments of the business.)

15

Kate Kelly

I don't think extensive research is needed to work out that the policy which seems to imply that local and community demand for live theatre is no longer alive and well, is unsupported by the real acid test; bums on seats. The additional proliferation of amateur productions and an outpouring of local talent would seem to be proof positive of that. Ken Dodd, a sell out where ever he plays, promised over five years ago, that if Barnsley could provide such a theatre, he would not only add it to his tour list; but volunteer to become a patron, bringing half a dozen 'bigger names' with him.

The sad fact remains; those areas which struggle to provide venues seating three to five hundred people are limited financially to the level of performer they can afford. You wouldn't really think that any town with a history of live entertainment would ever be without a theatre to perform in, but that did happen to many towns in the second half of the last century. It is true that it was an era of change with more modern, slicker gaming and theatre clubs emerging, in the changing face of entertainment of the 1960s; and there are those who still argue that there is no call in the town for live entertainment. That however doesn't quite equate with the fact that no less than three independent theatre groups have been born out of this same community, in defiance of that stand; two of them having their own premises. That is notwithstanding the proximity of Leeds, Bradford, Sheffield, Wakefield, Huddersfield, Doncaster and Rotherham, each with their own larger venues.

The Lamproom Theatre was the first. In 1998 John Kelly, a local free-lance journalist and former Grimethorpe collier, purchased one of Barnsley's oldest buildings. Built in 1792, on the site of the town's medieval 'Pen-Fold', the Westgate property served as the community's first Methodist Chapel. It was then a school before becoming 'Barnsley Boys' Club' in the 1950's, across the road from what any man over 60 will tell you was the 'real' Barnsley Old Boys' Club; now sadly demolished, the Black Bull Inn.

Kelly had previously chaired 'The Theatre Royal Trust' whose sole objective had been to purchase and restore the nineteenth century theatrical jewel located on Wellington Street. Unfortunately, the Theatre Royal was transformed into a Theme Pub and the trust duly lapsed into temporary dormancy.

Kelly however gathered several individuals who had participated in the 'Theatre Royal' project and proposed that they should redirect their efforts into providing the town with a much needed theatre. This, he argued, could be achieved by refurbishing the former Boys' Club. The Trust was renamed; Barnsley Theatre Trust (1998) Ltd. and, with the little residue of money from their previous venture and a loan from Kelly, the trustees and a small army of volunteers transformed the drug den dereliction into The Lamproom Theatre.

The Lamproom – named as such to commemorate the community's proud connection with the coal mining industry – opened its doors in the spring of 1999 and was, with its begged, borrowed and renovated equipment, a testimony to the inventiveness, tenacity and energy of the volunteers.

Working without grants or remuneration, Lamproom volunteers bought into the project for the theatre's future development. The town, following the demise of The Globe Theatre in the 1980s, had lost its former amateur dramatic societies; The Playgoers Society, The Junior Operatic Society and Barnsley Children's Theatre Company. For the Lamproom to make early progress it needed to regenerate local companies and stop using the word, amateur.

The Lamproom Theatre Company was formed and, with its eclectic mix of non-professional and semi professional personnel, became the town's first 'Community' theatre company. The Lamproom Youth Theatre Ensemble (LYTE's) quickly followed and a junior section, 'The LampLYTEr's, was created to satisfy an enormous public demand for child based performance related activities. Local Operatic societies relocated to the theatre following the closure of the Civic Hall and, by the end of the year, the Lamproom had recreated a thriving community theatre base within the town centre.

Without substantial grants the ever growing team of theatre lovers worked tirelessly to create and maintain substantial seasonal programming. Their efforts were rewarded when, after five tough years, the theatre-going population voted with their feet. Sell-out performances became commonplace and the project finally began to cover many of its costs.

Prior to the Lamproom's existence, John Kelly had written, *Randal's Scandals* with his friend and colleague, Keith Clifford – Billy Hardcastle of *Last of the Summer Wine* fame. The play, produced by former 'Barnsley Globe Theatre' Chairman, Roger Walton, enjoyed a highly successful twenty week British tour with, 'The Secret Theatre Company' later reformed as 'Barnsley's Secret Theatre Company' to present professional work and Christmas Pantomimes within the Lamproom. The company returned to touring in 2006 with, *Sparkies* by John Kelly and

The Lamproom became the first theatre in Barnsley to produce and promote professional touring theatre.

Kelly is quick to identify the man whose energy, initiative, enthusiasm, dedication and vision deserve absolute credit for saving the concept of live theatre in Barnsley. Roger Walton's tireless devotion to the Globe Theatre is what gave youngsters like Jonathan Ellis, Jeremy Peaker, John Hudson and Kate Kelly first their grounding, and then a direction to aim for to enable them to fly free. Kelly recognises Walton's insistence as being his own driving force to form the trust that eventually resulted in the Lamproom.

Between the two and countless others, performers, volunteers, donors and patrons they have created, contributed to and developed a truly remarkable community venture. Perhaps that is why The Lamproom is known locally as 'The People's Theatre'.

The newer Academy Theatre followed, modern and of similar size and accessibility. Its natural emphasis on song and dance is due to the experience and inherent strengths of its co-owners Geoff Whitfield and his daughter Julie Cooper. Their business is a combined theatre, music centre and school of dance, modelled ' . . . on Sylvia Young Theatre School lines; we're a sort of Northern version of that.' Whilst offering 'fun courses' for children whose interest is enjoyment in the experience, they also provide a structure for accredited courses. These are courses designed for the Performing Arts, Dance Drama and Music – to my ears. I see it as especially relevant in light of the current decimation of training provision for skills which offer alternative means of expression and communication.

'We have four hundred children from the age of three straight through to GCSE equivalent in the subjects, which offers more than just an experience of live theatre for those who want that,' Julie Cooper tells me. Their input fills a gap which will undoubtedly widen as increasing numbers of higher education colleges and universities drop the training of school teachers in these areas. The knock-on effect of that will obviously mean a shortage of teachers in these subjects not currently fashionable – or financially productive.

The theatre's programme of productions continues to belie the lack of demand or support and invariably sold out performances draw even wider geographical audiences.

2006 saw the emergence of Vibe Theatre Company with its ambitious production of an original play *No Horizon* performed entirely by local actors and based on the life of Penistone born genius Nicholas Saunderson. Losing his sight in the first year of his life, the child received little formal education, but he taught himself to read by moving his fingers across letters engraved on tombstones in the local churchyard.

The real Billy Elliott – Philip Mosley, at the preview of 'No Horizon' with David Blunkett, Max Reid and James Lomas – one of the boys who has played Billy Elliott in the West End production. *By kind permission of Marc Wilmot of Motography*

An amazing natural talent for mathematics finally won him a place at Cambridge where ultimately following Sir Isaac Newton, he became Lucasian Professor of Mathematics. Carefully researched writing and slick marketing by Andy Platts and Max Reid respectively, were backed by a range of the best local acting talent, and local choreographer Suzanne Grand. With a committed team of their supporters, Vibes' premier of the production at the Paramount Cinema, a miraculous reminder of what cinema used to be, put Saunderson's home town straight back onto the map. Their sheer hard graft and commitment absorbed audiences who felt they lived the story through the quality of the presentation, gaining the venture spontaneous support. With a co-production at the Sheffield Lyceum theatre already in the pipeline their ultimate dream of a West End production might not be just a dream. They already have the moral support of Tony Field CBE advising them; and his collaboration with Sir Paul McCartney in opening the Liverpool Institute for the Performing Arts of which he is Chairman, is no-one's pie in the sky.

The introduction of performing arts in schools made them great backup nurseries for spotting local talent and developing skills. Generations of Huddersfield's James Mason, Doncaster's Diana Rigg, Leeds' Peter O'Toole, Barnsley's Brian Glover and Kenny Doughty, Mexborough's Keith Barron, Goldthorpe's Brian Blessed and Sheffield's Sean Bean, Leeds' John Simm and Gaynor Faye. When backed up by the

Jonathan Ellis, currently appearing in the West End production of *Les Miserables* and Philip Mosley, Artistic Co-ordinator and character artiste at the Royal Ballet relax backstage at Covent Garden. *By kind permission of Tony Piggott – A.M.Photographic*

writing skills of the likes of Helen Fielding, John Godber, Barry Hines and John Kelly the list is endless. A Coronation Street hairdressing apprenticeship for Angela Griffin led to her cutting it elsewhere. The same school, Intake High in Leeds, also turned out Scary Spice for good measure. Sheffield's Tapton School had a different performer in Seb Coe, as did Silverdale School in England cricket captain Michael Vaughan, but it can also claim William Snape. Best known as Nathan, 'The Full Monty' child with more gumption than his dad, he later became Stephen Butler, one of many to fall in an Andy Sugden story line in Emmerdale.

Recognised by most people first for his comic portrayal of the suicidally gormless Lomper in *The Full Monty* the real Steve Huison takes acting to a much more serious level. Shipley based Shoestring Theatre Company, touring nationally with its production *Fifty Feet and Falling*, deals with depression and actual suicide winning unanimous acclaim from drama critics to health workers. Huison's nothing short of brilliant one-man performance takes the audience with him through a life from the age of nine year old innocence to disillusionment at fifty. In just one of many highlights he succinctly exposes the intricacies of adolescence in a brief solitary dance. The layers identified are followed up by expertly sensitive interaction with the audience led by partner

Theresa Smith. Having seen it done first as a local authority care initiative in Warrington, and then in a lighter 'an evening with' format, I can vouch for its amazing impact and quality at any level. Similar extremes are mastered within Shoestring's range of courses on offer, from a bridging project with Airedale Psychiatric Hospital stage to foundation training courses in clowning, Shakespearean acting, improvisation, voice and audition technique.

Susanne Grand was Steve's choreographer and the rest of the male strippers, including Leeds born Tom Wilkinson in *The Full Monty*. Creator of the cleverly understated dole queue dancing and through to the unforgettable finale, she scooped an American Choreography Award as well as an Oscar equivalent for Outstanding Achievement in a Feature Film, before returning to her Performing Arts Studio in Barnsley. Born in Grimethorpe Gary Clarke broke the mould when he became a freelance choreographer of contemporary dance, but is still umbilically linked to the area's history. Fourteen years after his appearance in *Children of the Dark* his company Pit Fleur plans a return to his origins with its newest project. He is creating a full length contemporary dance work which will focus on the physicality of coal miners. Aptly the work's September 2007 showcase is scheduled at 'the people's theatre' in Barnsley, the Lamproom Theatre, before embarking on a national tour in spring 2008. Local interest already high may be a barometer of its potential success.

Also from Willowgarth High School in Grimethorpe, Shaun Dooley became a baddie in *Coronation Street*, and a goodie in *Eastenders* and just about everything else in *Holby City*, *Peak Practice*, *The Grand*, *The Bill*, *Casualty*, *Silent Witness*, *Dalziel and Pascoe*, *Rosemary and Thyme*, *Strictly Confidential Shackleton* and even *Crossroads* long before *Mark of Cain*. You might also have spotted *Look North* capturing his performance as a history teacher twenty years after the strike. He was actually recounting his memories as a child at school during that period; but to twelve year olds that's history.

Gary Clarke. *The Author*

Sister Stephanie Dooley, in a move from a highly successful singing career gives short but effective shrift as the secretary temp who would take dictation but not much else from Emmerdale's King brothers. Jonathan Ellis once a transvestite in *Eastenders*, became a twin in 'Blood Brothers' amongst other leading roles in the West End before showing Kevin Kline a clean pair of dancing heels in big screen musical *De-Lovely*. Sheffield comic Bobby Knutt started out with Stan Richards in Ken Loach's *The Price of Coal* and had a staggering credit listing in TV before appearing in *Emmerdale* as a Dingle – Uncle Albert. And there's more to the 21st century's answer to Joan Collins, than the semi-naked Tanya Turner ever revealed. The girl who spent three weeks on a visit to the Dalai Lama, Huddersfield's Zoe Lucker, arguably invented the WAG in her searing *Footballers Wives* performance. As a toned down londe she revealed yet more in acting skill in *Holby City* as a far less glamorous but also less menacing single mum.

The latest entertainer to hit the small screen and the big Street, which incidentally was once produced by Barnsley lass, Suzi Hush, has a less glamorous role so her Becky may be less forgivable than the murderous Tanya Turner. Katherine Kelly is also a consummate actress I find, since she too is nothing like the character she portrays. 'I do know her and understand her though.' she tells me.

Drenched in the theatre and like her mother, loving musicals for as long as she can remember, she did tap, modern and ballet from the age of three. It was an odds on favourite that Kate Kelly would follow her

John Kelly with daughter Kate as Daddy Warbucks and Annie. *The Kelly family collection*

parents Anne and John Kelly on to the stage. Her first starring role *Annie* with her dad playing Daddy Warbucks confirmed she had ability. She had a long journey through many staging posts before getting that top billing, evidencing boundless enthusiasm and unflagging energy whilst gaining experience in as many local societies as she possibly could. Drama was not available as a GCSE subject at Wakefield Girls' High School, but she was additionally coached for her A level music recital in singing by Catherine Williams, the wife of a teacher at the school. 'She really has a superb singing voice,' is the unsolicited opinion I am given when mentioning her name in the school that has shared every step of her way. Those sessions taught her that she also had the necessary commitment. 'I didn't have one teenage Saturday. Instead it was two buses there and two back and working together all day, but worth every minute because that is when I learned to sing, really sing I mean; up to then I had just been copying what others did.'

She was backed by Headteacher Pat Langham's far-sighted decision to accept that eight weeks touring with the 'Secret Theatre Company' in her father's play *Randall's Scandals* was appropriate work experience. So at the age of seventeen she was able to experience touring, do auditioning, and study to take three subjects successfully at A level. John Kelly says he gave her no quarter on that tour, determined to show her the toughest side of life as an actor. 'It's just a blur now,' she says, 'it was so hectic. But it did show me the worst side of the business, and I couldn't believe how much I loved it despite all that.' So it seems physical and mental endurance as well as determination had to go on the list too.

Convinced that her ambition was a realistic option whilst others were discussing teaching as a career with a starting salary of £20,000, her response was predictable. 'I'd be euphoric to get that much for acting.' Applying to the Royal Academy of Dramatic Art, the Academy of Live and Recorded Arts, and Webber Douglas Academy, she was accepted by all three, so talent was clearly a factor too. She went for her first choice RADA and loved that too. It was there that Tim Piggot Smith told her, 'Don't lose the accent! It will make you a lot of money'. She kept that in mind discarding conflicting advice, 'Don't be precious with the accent dear . . .'

Three years later, at twenty-one she made a three year plan. Whirlwinding into 'a pretty mixed bag' for her first three parts in mini rep, she started at the Theatre Royal in York, *The Blue Room*, *Midsummer Night's Dream* and *Dangerous Liaisons*. From there it was on to Chichester with *Pals* then *Othello* at Manchester Royal Exchange. She kept up her contact with the Lamproom Theatre, taking part whenever she could and with panto leads in *Aladdin 2002* and *Jack and the*

Kate Kelly in the Lamproom production of 'The Boyfriend.' *The Kelly family collection*

Beanstalk in 2003. Her first TV job was *Sons and Lovers* filmed on the Isle of Man, which she thought was great, but her favourite of all her early TV work was *Silent Witness*. 'I played a sports agent in that, loved it, especially working with Amanda Burton. I learnt more on that TV job than any of the others I did until *Coronation Street*. She also had a part in *Last of the Summer Wine*. Roy Clarke OBE is so well loved for that Holmfirth-based comedy, it is sometimes forgotten that in his amazingly successful career amongst other work he has also written *Open All Hours* and *Keeping up Appearances*.

Kate Kelly kept up her appearances; theatrically for the first year, the set plan of television the second year and moved to Stratford and the Royal Shakespeare Company for the third. 'I was so thrilled I went back to school to tell them but was too late; Mrs Langham had already got the posters up in the hall!' A four play cycle meant the hardest work she had ever done. With no previous experience of playing the guitar for her first part, the title role in *Tamar's Revenge* meant guitar lessons from scratch during the day in addition to rehearsing, if not doing matinees, before evening performances six nights a week. The thirteen hour days were bad enough but she also learnt the impact of some roles. 'Tamar is such an emotionally draining part to play; being raped and then murdering your attacker every night.' She was run down and exhausted, but would not allow her parents to find out. 'You'd have had me out of there in a flash', she tells her dad when he reacts on hearing the account for the first time.

They were the best of times and the worst of times for her, 'but in terms of experience, unparalleled'. An unplanned move but one she loved was three weeks in Madrid, a part of the RSC contract playing in English with rolling subtitles. 'Spanish women were always allowed to play on stage, unlike England in the early days of theatre, so women's roles there were good leads, written for women not men playing women.' They also followed the RSC tradition of performing in Newcastle prior to taking the plays to the West End for a three month run. 'Fantastic!' is her summing up of that first experience. She has no sign of any off stage airs and simply rattles off a finger counting list of what else she has already done, '. . . a couple of films, a cheese advert and bits of TV, and I have been lucky enough to work with some great actors, but . . .' she had reached a plateau and felt that she had a choice to make. 'Actors age quickly, by your late twenties you're too old for Tamar – or Juliet'.

She had actually already exceeded her expectations, had big critical

Then Bishop of Wakefield, Nigel McCullough with one child from each of the 31 colliery communities scheduled to be closed in 1993. Just visible in the centre space of the back row is Elizabeth Peacock MP. *The Author*

acclaim and with a new agent found herself moving straight in to the fast lane and *Coronation Street*. 'I was terrified on the way there the first day, but I couldn't believe how friendly everyone was and so helpful, I loved it'. I am less surprised, reminded of my time working in a school in Grimethorpe just after the pit closed. In trying to motivate that generation of girls to widen their perspective and go for their dreams, I organised an International Women's Day link. Asking the girls to identify women in jobs they thought were proof of success, I then wrote to every one asking them to help encourage these girls to break through the glass ceiling. The response was amazing as photographs, letters and prizes came pouring in. Several, but not all, women Members of Parliament replied and one, Elizabeth Peacock, then Conservative MP for Batley and Spen, not only visited the school but arranged for two of the girls, prospective journalists, to visit both Houses of Parliament. All the Gladiators, (remember them?) replied with signed photos as did the Prime Minister of Norway. 'It's those lads again,' came the weary explanations as replacement copies of Jet and Lightning's photos were nicked from the display boards several times a day. I was gratified to note that the Prime Minister of Norway remained intact. Betty Eggleston and Kim Tate from Emmerdale sent prizes as did Katy Oxo (remember when Linda Bellingham was her?) Noticeably not only did virtually every female member of the cast of Coronation Street respond, but the then producer Carolyn Reynolds and members of the production team wrote personal letters too. Away on holiday for the weeks before the event, Sue Nicholls actually rang the school to apologise for not replying,

Original Calendar Girl Lynda Logan, now one of Becky's biggest fans, has watched Coronation Street fan since close friend Ernst Walden first appeared as Elsie Tanner's son-in-law, Ivan Cheveski. Though now living in Austria he visits their beautiful Dales home whenever he can. *By kind permission of Terry Logan*

and offered to come and visit at some time in the near future. It spoke volumes to those girls at that time.

Kate Kelly took to heart the advice that Bradley Walsh gave her on her first morning, 'Show them what you can do to make the part your own'. 'It was clear Becky was so damaged by life that she would be volatile, unreliable and aggressive. I thought she would be a cider-drinker, and I gave her the ever-present chewing gum or a fag in her mouth as well.' Kate's short term contract was one month into the story-line when the ending was re-written and her contract was extended. She is on target now with a new contract and the potential to become one of those incomers we hate, but then grow to love. Such characters have always been a big part of Corrie's strength and appeal. Though sub-sequently canonised, Elsie Tanner by 1950s standards was every bit as bad a mother as Cilla in 2007. The irascible Ena Sharples was the busy-body and the gossip that Norris is today; The Ogdens, MacDonalds, Malletts and Battersbys with their topical problems, 'vulgarity' and 'a lowering of standards . . .' were all initially berated by fans or critics, or both. Each in turn has played a part in not simply reflecting society, post event, but slickly forecasting potential changes in it. Becky's behaviour is now the subject of such philosophical debates nationwide, in the remaining post office queues, corner shops and small hairdressing salons – well it is mine! Since meeting Kate Kelly I find myself in the ridiculous situation of wanting to mitigate and even excuse the worst of Becky's behaviour in such discussions.

'Playing in Coronation Street is an unbelievable experience; one of the five things you have to do in your life,' she thinks aloud, so I press her for the other four in her own life. 'I'd quite like to do a voice over for

Chris Evans getting 'Up and Under' advice from author John Godber. *The Author*

an animation film; work with Kay Mellor; and maybe something to do with Harry Potter.' Before I can tell her that's only four she is talking about the 'unfailing support' that helped her keep on track in her steadfast ambition. She cites her parents and family; Wakefield GHS as the most caring school ever and everyone else at the Lamproom Theatre; but Chris Evans in particular. 'Everywhere, absolutely everywhere I have worked I have met someone saying it was Chris Evans who inspired them.'

Kate Kelly talks of the luck she's had, working with 'excellent actors and directors.' She cites the opportunities she had to play in semi professional theatre from an early age. I feel compelled to point out that opportunities have to be taken and there's no doubt luck is always a factor, but rarely beats a combination of the qualities her record to date flags up. Through hard work she has done very well, but is not 'a celebrity'; not of the kind claimed by today's sad standards. That she may become an actor whose performance and standards merit celebration is another matter. That possibility may already be borne out by the fact that she is welcomed back in her former school; not as an increasingly successful famous actor, but as a positive role model. So bearing in mind her weekly appearances on the street it's rather odd to hear that despite wearing little make-up she is rarely recognised as Becky off screen. 'Everybody hates Becky at the moment,' she says, and I, a life-long Corrie fan, silently wonder if I'm hearing a clue in there. She moves on telling me that fifteen minutes into a pleasant interview at her bank recently she was asked for details of her occupation. Replying that she was with Granada TV she was pressed further, so said she worked on 'Coronation Street'. Still not spotted she was asked what she did there, production, writing, make-up or what? She explained she was Becky and giggles at the reaction of disbelief. 'Everybody looks at me in a different way once they realise I'm her,' says an attractive, intelligent, self-composed and charming young woman – who clearly isn't type cast.

16

Susan Johnson

Once upon a time the stories told in school reports rarely had a beginning, middle or an ending, and equally infrequently required customised analysis of the abilities of individual children. At best they were a jolly encouragement, at worst a punitive exercise in delayed discipline. Some had the merit of one-liner wit, as one for a boy who systematically broke every piece of equipment he was given to work with in a Craft Department with which I worked in the 1970s. A teacher, clearly influenced by Winston Churchill's famous wartime speech 'Give us the tools and we'll finish the job' reported, 'We gave him the job and he finished the tools.' Another mused, 'Has set himself an abysmally low achievement target, and failed to achieve it.' Unhelpful in terms of target setting then, they are used now only as punch lines in sit coms like *Grange Hill* or *Byker Grove* or as after dinner speech nose-thumbs by the recipients.

Gloriously successful woman, and broadcaster, Jenni Murray still recounts one of her own reports from a history teacher in Barnsley, with a just a touch of glee, 'Jenni's attitude to facts is so cavalier she should consider a career in journalism.' Boom, boom! She had the determination and the confidence to over-ride its superficiality and take it as encouragement to do what she intended to do anyway. But what is most gratifying in my view is that it is not her imagination, tenacity or even her exquisite voice, but her attention to factual detail that makes Jenni Murray the outstanding BBC journalist that she undoubtedly is.

In a three page report in the August 2006 edition of *Vogue*, the sheer genius of Yorkshire born Josh Wood was seen through the eyes of his A-List celebrity clients. It made me think back to a report he told me he was given as a work experience student at the end of his year 11 placement in a hair dressing salon years earlier. 'Find yourself a different career lad; you're never going to make it as a hairdresser!' Currently more amusing than it was to the aspiring colourist some twenty years ago, he now accompanies some of the biggest names in show business on their world tours, and is routinely flown from his Realhair base in Chelsea by private jet to clients across the world. It is virtually impossible to visit the salon without a celebrity experience.

It's often interesting to find out what effect on people similar feed back has had, or the effect of those school reports which simply said,

'Satisfactory' or 'Must try harder.' Susan Johnson still remembers those very words with a wry smile. Throughout primary school reports had annually described her as a good, keen worker, and she smiles, 'really meaning one who was no trouble'. Not inspiring but good enough to leave her thinking that maybe she was good enough to stay on in the sixth form at Barnsley Girls' High School. Ironically the later, 'try harder' version went home at a time when she was emotionally and financially supporting four younger siblings, a sick mother and an absent father as well as being the first member of her family to study for A levels. When I ask if she thinks it resulted in her becoming what she clearly is, a self-critical workaholic, she nods vigorously, describing herself as 'driven' by a need to achieve. And achieve she has, quite remarkably, to be what she currently is, the first ever female, non-uniformed Chief of a UK Fire and Rescue Service.

Educating girls as late as the 1970s remained a low priority in many working class families, and a no-go option in others. So it was with her, and six months into her A Levels, due to her mother's ill health and subsequent inability to cope with the family alone, Susan Johnson had to abandon the course and all her dreams and aspirations, to look after her mother and her younger siblings. 'It was tough, but only because although I invariably had this 'ability average' rating, I always had this feeling that I could do better.' There were good role models around in the family, a music teacher on her mother's side and an American Space Project Programmer on her father's, but contact was infrequent and did not present encouragement, support or fostered ambition. Having left her A Level studies at the age of sixteen, just a year later she avoided the long-term threat of being just a second mother to her family, only to join the ranks of girls who marry too young.

Moving to the North East with her husband, she found herself without the extended family support she herself had provided, when she became a teenage mother. Like many of us who grew up feeling we were trained for nothing better, pin money jobs were for her the first rung on a sig-nificant ladder. Starting as a butcher's assistant, she worked throughout her first pregnancy. After the birth she took a job as a supermarket cleaner from 6.00 to 8.30 every morning, before her husband left for work, and again in the evenings after he came home. Not much of a change really, but what was changing generally was a growing aware-ness amongst girls like her that they did have options. School failures became late entrants to a range of training and learning opportunities as girls woke up to increasingly accessible reality; re-read Jane Austen maybe, but certainly began to accept that 'it's never too late to be what you might have been.'

For nine months she did a job she hated, but as a natural pragmatist made a decision. 'I'm totally bemused by people who spend a lifetime complaining about their jobs' she tells me, 'If you don't like what you do, do something about it!' What she did was to harness the skills and experience she was developing in her working life to leapfrog the A Level blockage. Realising that it was more of a psychological one than anything else in her case, she embarked on a two year HND Diploma in Business Studies at Sunderland Polytechnic and then from there to study for a BA Honours in Business and Finance.

The first class results she received there were her first undeniable confirmation that she did have ability. Moving on to a job with IBM, she recalls a feeling of being both successful and happy for the first time in her life. With it came growing awareness that aspiration was normal and ambition was realistic. I love her 'can do' philosophy and her easy recognition of applying intellect and work ethic to reach goals. Her second child was six months old when she gave up her job, and on a part-time basis, did another leapfrog to undertake a Masters Degree course at the esteemed University of Durham. 'It was made a bigger decision because it was decided that I had made myself voluntarily unemployed, so I was not entitled to a grant for the two and a half years it took,' grins an unstoppable pragmatist.

The ladder she was now on was not to a job, but to a career. The perspective and overview from that height was better. 'During my career in the private sector I was acutely aware that in many businesses' success or failure could depend on the economic climate, the help they received from public agencies and their inability to assess global market trends. This is how I got interested in economic development and prompted my move to head up the Northern Business Forum', she explains. Highly rated and happy as she was there, she applied for and was appointed as Executive Director for Business Development with Yorkshire Forward. I recall the celebratory announcement in the *Barnsley Chronicle* at the time, and the little stir as this local girl joined the ranks of those overcoming odds and making good. 'I was appointed as I had relevant private sector experience combined with what they saw, as an understanding of business,' she says. 'It was how it should be, the fact that I was a woman was never an issue there; all that mattered was that I could do the job.'

She clearly has a happy nostalgic feeling for the six challenging but rewarding years she spent there. Her record continues to speak for her in the warmth of everyone's recollections of her. Team creation and a plethora of leading skills styles and management is a great legacy she left. She omits to tell me that she was awarded an Honorary Scholarship by Sunderland University and then an OBE. When I raise it she grins again, 'Other Buggers' Efforts, that's what they say about honours you know.' Of course I do, and in many cases they are right, but not in hers, as I am reliably informed by her former colleagues. I feel the need to ensure that she knows this too and press the point, asking if she still has hang-ups about that early 'average' label and the inbred sense of low self esteem. 'Oh definitely,' she agrees, 'I don't think I'll ever get rid of the feeling that I don't deserve anything.' She didn't even feel she deserved to celebrate going to the University to celebrate her Fellowship. She received it from Lord Puttnam in the company boardroom at two o'clock in the afternoon, sandwiched between two business meetings in a usual full working day. A day incidentally, which typically included her recognition of the achievements of six other people by presenting them with Community Awards. Naively I ask her if she regards these achievements as her own best; and I get the answer I should have anticipated. 'To date . . . .' She isn't in any way conceited, self-praising or pushy, she is just driven.

Her present position is not a gender bias free zone, but the territory of uniformed men. With a job description that includes Chief Fire Officer she is at the top of an extending ladder, of dizzier heights and precarious footing and one previously never scaled by a woman. Coming from the male dominated workforce area that she did, she knows well enough about the traditional challenges of such a shift. She was at first puzzled by what she saw as an initial reluctance to accept her other than as a woman doing a man's job. Increasingly, it became clear that she was actually in a male ego society in full bloom. She felt as if she was on a film set on her first morning on the job, which she had in part been given due to her previous record of showing that different styles of leadership work in getting best all-round results. I immediately visualised Helen Mirren, they are not dissimilar in appearance actually, but I was wrong again.

She arrived at the red-coned car park to be greeted by a saluting doorman who called her 'Ma'am'. On asking what his name was and being answered very formally, she said, 'Good morning Peter, my name is Susan, would you call me that in future please?' The next morning she was greeted in the original way and again pointed out that she preferred to be called by her first name. The film set I begin to realise, was not *Prime Suspect* or even *Towering Inferno*, but *Groundhog Day*. So after three days of the same ritual, she told him with mock severity that his failure to carry out a simple instruction could become a sackable offence. A further three week breaking-in period of her being called 'Ma'am' followed, before he was able to relax into calling her 'Mrs'. She accepts that for old and ingrained practice to change is not easy, but insists that to bring the service into line effectively with at least some now recognised aspects of good management is crucial.

'It was surreal in my experience, as was the way that all office doors were permanently closed and entry was by invitation only.' Her open-door style and cards on tables was set out for the entire service. 'I kept the door to my office open throughout the nine months it took before anyone came in without an appointment!' she tells me with a touch of sadness. I have a sudden thought that she is in the service which has poles intended to slide people down as quickly as ladders to help them up.

Such tenacity and her questioning of what she regards as out-of-date and constrained patterns of behaviour can be seen as provocative. 'Is it possible to have a modern fire service in a hierarchical system?' She grins again, adding that she has now been given a name that they all use behind her back – Miss Chief. I ask her if she thinks she may be ahead of her time, and get the quick-draw fire back, 'No but I'm ahead of theirs!' She reflects on a self-appraisal she carried out after fourteen months in post. 'I estimate that 300% more input has generated one tenth of improvement in output when compared to my last job.' She has a great concern that the entire service is not yet in a mind-set for effective change and that there is little to no appetite for modernisation. There are such conflicting internal factions; a cherished brave heroism that society loves and deserves, and is at risk of needing more and more, set against an outdated undercurrent with political priorities and childish initiation ceremonies. 'The officers who put their lives on the line are, and should be well paid, but I don't see recognition of inter-dependence across the service. What I do see is the divisiveness of 12% pay increases against 2.7% for others.' What they see is a non-operational woman running their public tax-funded archaic service and they can't wait to see her fail.' I have another sudden thought that poles can be greased.

It is tough talking, but it reflects the measure of the woman in no small way. She looks and sounds pleasantly engaging, pretty and blonde! But as I said, she is a lot like Helen Mirren; has a mind like a steel trap and I'd say, does not suffer persistent fools gladly. On one occasion before I met up with her at one of her highly valued business training sessions, I sneakily asked a couple of men just out of the sessions what they thought of her performance. 'Well it's not a performance,' said the first, 'she justifies everything she says and you know you are listening to someone who can deliver the goods as well as the programme.' 'She is totally honest,' said the second, 'her views are balanced, based on sound judgement and I would trust her implicitly, even if I didn't agree with her!'

Waiting back at the ranch is her preferred option, of being an informal colleague who effectively manages a united and efficient modern public service team. Still on the back boiler, simmering away is another agenda, as she continues to undertake fire fighting of a different order. I ask her if it is all worth it and for the first time she hesitates. 'It is emotionally draining to have to constantly watch your own back, but I am resilient, don't need to be loved and moving on holds no fears for me.' As I wonder what ladder she will stand on next, and why this one suddenly doesn't look as high is it did from the ground, I see the shape taking a different, three dimensional form. Height, like gender doesn't matter to her, not when added to a broad depth of experience and a perspective as wide as hers. The sky is the limit and she didn't start the fire.

17

Simon Hirst

You can't quite get your head round it; you're having lunch in Barnsley, in the little café in Pollyanna, sitting face to face with a guy who tells you he has just come from interviewing Paris Hilton. I'm gossipy curious to know what she is really like, and how they got on, she of the hotel line that Elizabeth Taylor married into first time around, and he of Athersley North. 'She's very nice,' he responds cagily, but I know from the eyes that he is simply being the ultimate professional. I bet she loved him. She 'just lurved' everything and every-body else he asked her about in the interview as I discovered later listening to it on his website. I try a Pink comparison to draw him, but I quickly guess that on that particular subject I was going to get no more out of him than he got out of Paris. It wasn't a provoked Nicole Kidman or Meg Ryan shutters up job against him though, I suspect it was rather that she just doesn't have anything else to say. Nor does he on that one!

He has something to say on anything else though; he loves talking, does it well and shows interest in everyone else and everything they say. What he doesn't know about he readily admits and then comes back with question after question until he feels he does know more about it. We are dropping big names, a favoured mode of mine, so I trump his Robbie Williams with David Attenborough whose own favourite inter-view was with Australian 'top man' TV presenter and chat show host Andrew Denton. 'There is no question with him of it being 'My Show' or trying to make himself look good, it's all about bringing out the best in the person the interview is really about ' he once told me. 'He acknowledges them as the stars of the show. I admire his work immensely.' Denton's greatness it seems is based on a considerable intellect being focussed entirely on drawing out the interviewee, so that they feel at their very best. I agree having already come across Denton's work in a cracking interview he did with Dr Fiona Wood, just after she became Australian of the Year.

You can already hear a similar kind of quality in Simon Hirst despite it being of a totally different genre, and with a very different target audience. I don't think he has spotted it himself, but instinctively he is saying the same thing as Noel Coward, 'there is nothing as potent as cheap music.' He uses it as a vehicle for sharing his love of music whilst requiring mental responses from his audience. He exudes a bubbling enthusiasm which has networked more than a hundred and fifty independent radio channel links connecting him and the latest top forty hit tunes to innumerable young ipods every Sunday afternoon. He is young still, to be so adept in pleasing the fleeting fickle taste of the Top Forty audience, but has a personal taste in music that transcends pop.

He quotes his all-time favourite song, Joel's *Scenes from an Italian Restaurant*; and closely follows it with another piano man, Scott Joplin's *The Entertainer*; and I go for Joel's *Keeping the Faith* and Tony Bennett's *When Joanna Loved Me*. It is an old one he has never heard, so he immediately jots it down to listen to later. We share raves about the sheer brilliance of Joel's lyrics, then Bennett's phrasing comparing it to Sinatra and Ella Fitzgerald. We pepper through four decades lost in let's remember, picking out our best remembered and almost forgotten. I'm delighted as he likens the phrasing, pitch and timing of the best of popular music to the comedy timing of such greats as Kenneth Horne, The Goons and Tony Hancock. He understands perfectly why I have watched Ken Dodd do his live on stage marathons for over fifty years without once being bored, and why I still have an LP of Spike Milligan's poetic *Muses with Milligan*.

If the measure of a powerful person is that their circle of influence is greater than their circle of control, I am even more delighted to find

Billy Joel declares his interest in the Grimethorpe Book in a Day. *By kind permission of Paul Drabble*

159

someone of his age, and with his capacity to influence the young, who is totally committed to regeneration of towns in the area, and particularly Barnsley. As we talk about the economic climate in our home town I am actually using Joel's *Allentown* lyrics to encapsulate the outcome when towns lose their means of making a living; the stultification, apathy and wasted potential that ensues in schools and entire communities. He comments on the great use of language so I have to fess up that they are Joel's words not mine. He instantly admits he had always enjoyed the song but never spotted the analogy, or that it reflected the simultaneous reality of closure of thirty one pit towns and villages. Nor the death of the steel industry in Sheffield, the virtual closure of ports Newcastle, Hull or Liverpool, and the demise of a county's spinning and weaving history. He makes another note, to play it again and listen more carefully and adds Down Easter Alexa for good measure.

So I have to ask myself why, with such a natural thirst for knowledge and an appetite to do what it takes to learn, he tells me he was a total failure at school. He puts it down in part to the fact that as long as he could remember he was obsessed with an intention to become a DJ. 'From the age of ten I was already ringing DJs at Radio Aire, just to talk to them, and feel a part of it.' What he still cannot accept is that no-one at school seemed to realise that the intensity of his interest would be a basis for motivating him, 'I told everybody how I would spend hours creating my own radio programmes, and that was all I ever wanted to do.' He cracks up remembering he even wrote imaginary fan letters to himself so he could practise answering them 'for when the real ones started coming in.' Even worse no-one took seriously the possibility of that happening. 'There's only one Dave Lee Travis,' is the only career advice he can recall ever being given.

As it happens, he was not prepared to take that advice so just switched off. Clearly never going to 'grow out of it' he went on listening to the DJs of the day, James Whale, Fluff, Steve Wright, Kenny Everett and the rest. One of our meetings is the day after the news that Alan Freeman died, and he breaks the conversation, as if with a news flash, to recall momentarily what an inspiration and great master DJ the man was. His own standing in the industry is clear to me too when he mentions how good it felt that he was asked to contribute to Fluff's obituary.

Hirsty has an innate love of all kinds of popular music, but it is only recently, he tells me, that he feels he has the confidence to do something he would have loved to do at school, learn to play the piano. 'So I'm taking lessons and I won't stop until I'm good at it.' His own piano had been delivered that week he tells me so I ask if he can play anything yet.

Is this the youngest DJ on record?
The Hirst family collection

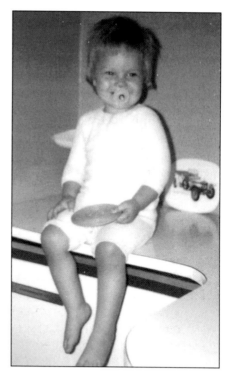

I shouldn't have really. I am totally unsurprised when he hums the first four lines of *Scenes from an Italian Restaurant* slowly playing an imaginary piano on the table cloth.

New London clients lunching there are pleasantly surprised but the regulars take it all in their stride. Josie, the most familiar of them explains that she has met lots of singers and dancers there. She has too, Royal Ballet's Philip Mosley, Gary Clarke 'he does very modern dancing' which he does but also choreography for his own company Pit Fleur. She has also met one of the Swing Out Sisters and Human League's Phil Oakey all in the last month. Hirsty grins explaining that it is places and people like this which will keep him with a foot on the ground in Yorkshire whatever else he does. The very next day the Prime Minister seems to be doing a u turn on the teaching of arts in schools, appearing now to see that 'Culture' is a pre-requisite for a rounded education, it's what we used call the arts I think.

Hirsty isn't one of education's real failures, ones who never knew they could want more out of life, or one of Billy Joel's won't be getting up today; he always knew how to survive with the dream. He listened, researched and from every available source he could find, taught himself skills he knew he would need, because his dream wasn't going to go away. Reel to reel cutting, splicing, mixing and voice-overs in his make-shift studio at home became his own highly successful Individual Education Programme over the next couple of years. In inverse pro-portion his effort and success, in terms of conventional education, nose-dived along with his flagging interest and ultimately his atten-dance. From being in the top two groups in his first year, he left school he says as 'one of the failures in the bottom groups.'

It's always the same in the end he learned, you never go back, but find a way to get by. His morale shot from low to high, as his school attendance was sacrificed to Radio Aire, where someone had spotted some potential in him, giving the twelve year old a chance to go into their studios and help out. He remembers those days hanging out but constantly learning, watching, listening and from people he admired and wanted to be as good as, not just to emulate. He had, of course, unwittingly invented the notion of self-motivated apprenticeship, work experience or maybe NVQ, and actually got on with it.

The big thing about being seen to be so far down the pecking order of potential is that, with any drive at all, the only way is up. He was less concerned with proving others wrong than proving to himself that he was right; and so began years of more effort, more development, more experience and more taken opportunities. For someone who was once excluded from school he demonstrates a strong sense of self disci-pline. He mentions a mutual friend who he knows from working out at the same gym as he does, a Hilton-linked one I note so I ask if that is how he gets to keep in good shape. There's no hint of an ego as he replies, 'No, I got fat. I was 14 stones and didn't like it so have got rid of it; well there's just a bit of double chin left now.' There isn't actu-ally, I note as he looks up to say 'Oh I'm having the roast oak salmon, salad and elderflower water again.'

He was still just a kid when he was asked to fill in on Radio Aire. He loved it, took to it like a fish to water but began to have this feeling that he could not shake off. 'Despite really appreciating everything done to help me there I was, and felt I always would be 'that kid who used to hang around' and I had to move on.' His research into his chosen subject had left him with Kenny Everett as a hero, and finding another

A happy truant. *The Hirst family collection*

162

great hero of his who shared the view, he made a demo tape and sent it to Paul Carrington at Minster FM. He can't identify now whether it was a burst of enthusiasm or a total lack of confidence, which at eighteen prompted him to hedge his bets and send the tape to Hallam FM and Pulse at the same time.

What he does know is that the tape was no good. 'There was a rawness about it that was evident, it was technically sound but I was still learning the art of pulling my own style together whilst just playing the hits.' All three rejections arrived at the same time. 'There's another lesson there about sending demo tapes off,' he cautions, 'stagger 'em so they don't all come back and hit you at the same time!' He was disappointed to be turned down by Hallam and The Pulse, but gutted to be turned down by Funster Paul Carrington as '. . . . not what I'm looking for'. He sat in a room of his own on the edge of the bed reading and re-reading the letter of rejection from a man who would later become one of his radio heroes, and decided he couldn't just accept it.

'I picked up the phone, rang him and asked if I wasn't what he was looking for, why wasn't I?' Carrington, who had started out his career as a helper for Timmy Mallett, with a young Chris Evans, seemed to be stopped in his tracks. 'Ok, come and do a live demo in the studio then,' was response to the initiative. 'I was completely fired up; I jumped in the Nova, bombed down the A64 to York and did a new demo straight off.' Carrington's response was really music to his ears, 'Why didn't you do it like that in the first place, you're on?' The next Sunday he was on air, on his own, live and following the *Chart Show*!

'I cut my teeth on Minster,' he tells me. 'I could see I had been just 'that kid' at Aire, an apprentice really, but now I was in a bigger league.' A sweet moment followed when, after two rejection letters, he was asked to join The Pulse. 'That's when I really began to bite' he recalls, telling me how he would be there in the middle of the night in the studio doing links and jingles in preparation for the show. So possibly that childhood 'obsession' was an unrecognised early indication of potential; of creditable professionalism or work ethic. Whatever it was in due course it brought acceptance from the third station that had originally turned him down, Hallam FM.

The Hallam contract was to do the 4pm to 7pm slot, presenting *Hirsty's Big Drive Home Show*. Live on air he heard the first announcement of the programme and then his voice saying, 'Hello, this is Hirsty,' and it felt good! He had a simultaneous flashback to school when he was sure nobody believed he could ever make it, and thought, '. . . some of 'em will be driving home listening to this, and now they know they got it wrong!' He thought he was the Duke of Earl riding around with the car top down and the radio on, got a good job, and got a new life. He really had thought he had made it when he got his photo in the *Barnsley Chronicle* after they did a profile on him. Seriously he tells me, these were dangerous times, 'Billy Joel's everybody loves you now moments, when you can get an attack of ego if you're not careful.' He says his attack lasted a few months but was abruptly cured when his mother told him he'd 'got a real ego', and his best mate called him 'Big Head' and said he was too cocky! More as a mental memo to himself, he adds that just in case he gets another attack he must never forget those days. I don't see any prospect of that happening with this young man. That Hallam moment was the buzz of justification. Everyone who has felt they carried the label of failure momentarily feels that same buzz when they do achieve some kind of success.

But after three very successful years at Hallam, and making his name in his home town, he decided it was time for him to do a breakfast show. He moved to Viking FM in Hull joined by Danny Oakes, aka Pimp Daddy Dog, 'a Royston stand up comic who used a strong American accent he had perfected, and then had to keep using so as not to disappoint the fans'. Success looked even more of a possibility when they won a Sony Radio Award for Broadcasting.

It gave Simon Hirst access to a world he had never imagined even in the fantasy days of writing his own fan mail. 'I met John Peel,' he says and it's enough. It is one of those iconic moments in lucky lives; to be

Simon Hirst, the legendary John Peel, producer Darren Lethem and Danny Oakes. *Simon Hirst's collection*

Ashley Jackson receives a Lifetime Achievement Award at the Yorkshire Awards ceremony in December 2006. *The Author*

in the same room as a legend. He's savouring not boasting in his total disbelief that he got an award at the same ceremony as John Peel got his Lifetime Achievement Award. 'He actually talked to me for fifteen minutes and he introduced me to Sheila the Pig . . . . !' His unbridled enthusiasm for Peel's achievements prompts me to ask what his own treasured moments are. 'Looking at a forty thousand fans at the Party in the Park in Hull; I picked out my own dad in the crowd. 'He'd played in bands himself, but never to forty thousand; it was such a buzz to see him there.'

He was right on time and on target next, across the region with Hirsty's Daily Dose in a Galaxy state of mind. He brought Danny with him, and together with JoJo, they have to date done four years of award winning ad libbing and just being themselves, in a very nice style. Things are ok with him these days but he is at a crossroad as we speak; realising that he doesn't want to spend half his week and life on a motorway working seven days a week. 'I've had the national profile, and loved it, but for now I really want a bit of time out to build a house with a studio of my own . . .' he thinks aloud as I ask him what now? He is grounded, well rounded, too lateral in his thinking to be obsessive, and would love to have kids. And he is too big a genuine fan

Hirsty and Robbie. *Simon Hirst's collection*

of others for that one attack of growing big to become a chronic condition; it was a learning curve and he is a good learner with an individual, if unusual, learning style. It is possible however that traces remain of that childhood absorption and thinking in terms of all things musical, which he'll never quite shake off. He is to be one of the celebrity guests at the Institute of Directors Yorkshire and Humberside Mayor's Charity Dinner at Brooklands Hotel and I ask if he wants to share a taxi. 'No thanks I won't need one, by car the run only takes as long as Piano Man . . . . !'

He talks movingly about the importance of being believed in and encouraged, particularly by his parents but also by others with professional integrity. Around 1992 he sought the advice of a famous professional DJ after hearing him say on TV that the young never seem to ask for advice any more. Hirsty did just that, writing and asking what he thought was the best way for someone with his experience to get further in the business. In return he tells me with disbelief he received a three page letter which amounted to a personal reference he treasures still, from Dave Lee Travis. 'They got that right then; there is only one Dave Lee Travis!'

Maybe not. Just days later, I'm on my way to Leeds for the 2006 Yorkshire Awards ceremony, where Ashley Jackson is to pick up a Lifetime Achievement Award. Driving us there is my pal for all his twenty one years, Ben Platts who asks if I and my pal for much longer than that Aileen Cook, mind if he puts the radio on for the news. We don't but hearing that it is tuned to Galaxy, I ask if that is his favourite station. You couldn't fix his reply if you tried. 'Sort of, but I always listen when Hirsty's on, he's hilarious. Everybody listens to him and I don't know anybody who doesn't like him. There's only one Hirsty!' Don't you just love the irony of that?

18

Fiona Wood

You really cannot call it a fair swap! We got the Female Eunuch from Australia, and they got Fiona Wood from Yorkshire. We finish up with chattering and classless Germaine Greer and they get the most amazing woman I have ever met. But as she says, 'Like they say, life's just a bazaar; it's how we cope with what it throws at us that matters.'

I first heard about Fiona Wood and her work with burns victims, from Calendar Girl Ros Fawcett, to whom I am eternally grateful. Ros is better known as Miss November, the witty knitter, whose modesty and much, much more, is concealed behind her knitting on photographer and artist Terry Logan's brilliantly witty calendar. The whole world now knows how it instantly and internationally transformed the image of the Women's Institute, and then immortalised six ladies of the Rylstone Branch, in the buff. She had heard about the incredible popularity and achievements of a Dr Fiona Wood, the Western Australian of the Year, from one of the doctor's good friends 'a very elegant and obviously seasoned traveller' sitting nearby on a plane as she jetted back from the Australian premiere of the film with Angela Baker. On being told that the doctor's accent was very similar to hers (so she's from Yorkshire obviously) Ros decided that I should include her achievements in this book and duly rang to tell me that as soon as she arrived back home. Despite that help I was unable to establish enough information to follow it through until some six months later, when Ros sent me a detailed newspaper article to put me back on the trail.

The trail would have to lead me on from a lot of happy days and a bit of work in Atlanta to Los Angeles where I met up with Stephen Moody and Tracy Wilkinson, to Perth Western Australia, where I was able to contact the surgeon at the Burns Unit of the Royal Perth Hospital. Busy as she clearly was Dr Wood agreed to see me, but regretted that she had no free time on her flying visits to Europe. What little spare time she had in England she told me, was always spent in Yorkshire with her mother, father and younger sister Nicola.

The day of our first meeting, the Yorkshire born Australian of the Year and I, starts at nine in the morning, or rather mine does. She had as usual begun at 5am with her customary swim in the Indian Ocean just across the road from her home in Perth, and sorted out the family and breakfast before completing a 6am Consultant's ward round in the

Burns Unit of the Royal Perth Hospital. She would not have left without checking on how each of her patients was, what overnight changes there had been for better or worse, and whose treatment might need adjusting in the three days she would be away from them.

I am soon to learn that you have to see her with one of her patients or ex-patients to understand what they mean to her and even more what she means to them. It isn't just her manner, the medical expertise, skill, or even the quality of time she gives them, it's much more. It is spirit and faith and strength and belief and hope and implicit respect and trust in the confidence that they have in her and take from her. Their use of words like unbelievable and genius is literal when speaking of her. She has an equally strong relationship based on mutual trust, loyalty and faith in the strength and spirit of the medical team she leads there, and whom, she repeatedly reminds me, are equally entitled to share the credit for the achievement of the Unit as she is.

By 7.30 that morning, whilst I had a bath and a leisurely breakfast in the hotel, she had attended a meeting which ran through to just before our allocated meeting time. I had never met her before, nor even seen a photograph of her, but through the thronged reception area of the hotel I watch her stride across the forecourt and instantly pick her out. She is smaller than I expected, Chanel-style suited, strikingly attractive; and looks both confident and relaxed as she walks purposefully towards me, with an out-stretched hand and a bright, beautiful smile of friendly greeting. 'We're ten minutes late already,' she tells me, 'so it could turn in to one of those days.' I can tell from her grin that whatever 'one of those days' might bring it won't throw her, and I should not let it throw me either.

'Is this you for three days?' she asks looking at my handbag, presuming a capacity of Mary Poppins' proportions. It is at this stage that I realise that her invitation means I am actually going to spend the weekend with her, not just grab a half hour from time to time when she can fit me into her constantly packed schedule. Faster than I have moved in years I hurl three days-worth of everything that I might need, or not need, into a bag; and she fills up with fuel for the 4WDl, and energy drinks and protein bars for us. As we set off I hear that our itinerary will be; a drive 'down south' to Busselton, check her in for the next day's Triathlon, make a couple of other visits and check into a nice hotel to stay for the weekend. I relax at the prospect of such an easy day with abundant time to get to know a little about her.

En route we stop to pick up Delia, her friend and cycling partner, and as we start the three hour drive south from Perth the triage talk is of tyres, times and tactics. Their interest in the event is intense, and equally intense are the competitive strategies they briefly discuss. Frequent interruptions are from hands-free incoming calls; a range of medical enquiries, the National Geographic Magazine wanting an interview, a second opinion on a development in the ward, or her opinion on this and that. She runs a reminder service of outgoing calls, what flowers her mother likes to be included in the bouquet she is ordering for her for Mothering Sunday, what each of the children will need to do and to have with them later in the day, ad infinitum. In between she begins to tell me what she thinks I might need to know. It is her treasured family upbringing, her early years in education and training, her passion for her work and the love she still has for Yorkshire despite her happy new life with her husband and children – as an Australian.

They prove to be an amazing and successful couple in their own right, her parents Geoff and Elsie Wood, and not just because, against the odds, they have produced even more successful children. The odds, it seemed, might have evened out a little when as a child, Geoffrey Wood passed to go to the local Grammar School in 1939. He couldn't take up the offer though, because the school uniform was too expensive. We know well some of the implications of those early well-intentioned class-merging experiments. My earliest recognition of it was one of Richard Attenborough's earliest film performances as the working class boy who took such a place in 'The Guinea Pig.' The inequality of such equality can bequeath a sense of shame as enduring as any joy of learning. Nearly sixty years later, whilst telling me that he went instead to the local school wearing clogs, Geoff Wood is remarkably unscarred, but he can still name the best-dressed boy in the class, the local butcher's son George Pacey. I remember being the only child not in full uniform in my first grammar school year. Elsie recalls different, but equally cringing days; 'my foster mother when I wanted a winter pixie hood like the others had, made one out of the sleeves of last year's coat.' But we do laugh at the some of the old class structuring of those days, as Geoff tells me of 'another lad, a really good football player, but from a family who couldn't afford studded football boots for him to play in. Someone bought him a pair, but his mother took them straight to the cobblers and had them soled and heeled.' Names such as Dan, Ike, Len and Bill were what the men in the Wood family traditionally called their sons. His mother preferred the 'more refined' Cyril and Geoffrey names she gave to her sons. 'Don't forget we lived in a mining village and my dad never got over it; as long as he lived he only ever called us Mick and Dick.'

They are beyond class now; the personification of self-education, developed intellect and achievement through hard work. She, finding inspiration in the training of the RAF, then made for herself a lifelong career in youth work and teaching, receiving personal commendation from Sir Alec Clegg for her inputs. He at the age of 14 left school and signed on at the Hemsworth and Featherstone Colliery Company, to work at South Kirby pit. 'We weren't educated, never mind being educators' he says, 'but if the (conveyor) belt broke we'd have to wait for it to be mended. Then we'd sit and talk; history, archaeology, books we'd read, in the only time we had to talk as men. There were some bright lads down pits in those days.'

I know he is right and I think you were wrong, Mr Giddy. Educating such children does not by definition lead to sedition and 'stations in life' disappeared about the same time as the rest of the best of the railway network. Opening schools opens minds and entitlement to education has led to the opening of doors to a totally different way of life, not just for individuals, but arguably, for the betterment of society in general. I love Geoff Wood's story of the VIP visiting his colliery who, commenting on the improved pay and conditions in mining, smilingly asked him if his two sons would be going to work at the pit with him. 'No they won't, because I've got this crazy idea, that one day I'll stand on a river bank cheering while I'm watching 'em row for Oxford or Cambridge.' I imagine the smile that would have earned on the day he said it. But these parents did not acknowledge boundaries in terms of achievement, so neither do their children or grandchildren. There are more grins now, as he tells how the genes go on, with not one of them ever considering losing as an option. Joe, one of Fiona's children, lost a wheel from his bike during a Triathlon, 'So Joe just picked up the bike and ran the rest of way with it. It would never have occurred to him to give up!'

Of the Woods' children, the youngest and only one still living in Yorkshire is Nicola, a vivacious, bright, enthusiastic young woman in education, currently one step away from the top rung of the state school ladder or hoop system. Her strength is aimed at ensuring better opportunities for children not gifted with determination, aspiration or even support. Geoffrey, the elder of their two boys, was a by-product of the disaffection caused by the imposed raising of the school leaving age in the early seventies. Refusing to go on to higher education he left without adequate qualification and joined the small but rapidly expanding new supermarket chain, Asda. He was successful and happy at the age of eighteen to become a trainee manager with them, until shop fitters arrived to do work at the branch. Discovering that they earned four times as much as he did, he upped sticks, left and with three others formed their own company – shop fitting!

Financially though not intellectually rewarding, the job did enable him to enjoy leisure time in London where, by this time his brother David was at university and Fiona was doing her training at St Thomas'. Occasionally standing in to play on David's rugby team he was bitten by the atmosphere, the fun and particularly the sport, realising what he

Geoff Wood, a winner. *The Wood's family collection*

had missed by his earlier rebellion against education. He set about learning with a voracious appetite, undertaking 'O' level examinations whilst working as a housemaster at a Borstal Young Offenders' centre. A keen boxer, he discovered what he viewed as a personal weakness, fainting at the sight of blood. Determination is a big genetic endowment in this family, so his response was to undertake work in the operating theatre of Pinderfields Hospital until he mastered it.

With a CISWO scholarship to further his studies he finally won a place at King's College, Cambridge, where he decided 'rowing was for toffs', but gained double honours for boxing. Geoff senior's grin lights up his face again as he recalls being punted across the Backs and by the lawns of Cambridge by a double blue, 'as proud as any toff!' Ever the rebel, the headstrong young Geoff Wood soon decided that his chosen course of Sociology was for 'trained monkeys' and switched to Law; graduating and succeeding first as a solicitor, then as a Crown Prosecutor, though his full potential was never realised. After a typically passionate Saturday afternoon rugby match, this remarkable young thirty three year old tragically collapsed and died at Pontefract Rugby Club. They tell me with equal pride of their surviving son, Professor David Wood, Professor of Surgery (Orthopaedics) at the QEll Medical Centre in Perth. Anyone studying total or hemiarthroplasty, giant bone tumours, patella resurfacing, the assessment of bone architecture or post hip fracture mortality, will tell you of the quality and influence of Professor Wood's research and practice. He will not.

As we drive south from Perth I find his sister, Fiona, strong, articulate, positive, questioning, and intelligent as she exudes integrity and enthusiasm in bubbles of humour occasionally laced with self-deprecation. There's not a trace of arrogance or false modesty, she knows what she has worked hard at in order to become good at it, and that her feet are firmly on the ground and will remain there, is crystal clear. There's a slight Ozzie upward inflection in her speech, but her vowels are as pure as the day she left Ackworth. She is open and forthright, telling me she knew would marry Tony Keirath the first day she saw him at a course for medical fellowship, and identifies the many strengths, qualities and attributes she saw in him. As she adds that he is also completely unflappable, I realise that she has just described herself, and wonder if she knows.

It's a three hour drive, and we are just still the ten minutes late as we arrive in Busselton, where I learn she is due to speak to two hundred women at their annual lunch. This then is one of the 'couple of visits' we were scheduled to do. She sprints ahead of Delia and me as the thought crosses my mind that with no public speaking element in her training, she might be nervous. By the time I have clambered down from the vehicle and we reach the building, I know how wrong I am, as the sound of laughter leads us to where she is. Already into her speech without ceremony or notes, Fiona Wood is telling them who she is, how it feels and what it entails to be a woman whose life now has changed beyond recognition since she became Australian of the Year 2005–06.

That's the first myth to go, because she leaves no-one in any doubt that she is not a solo performer, but part of a team, and privileged to be so. She has a mantra, which I'm hearing for the first time, born of a determined strength and genuine philosophy which you just know was hers before Bali and all the recognition that follows her incredible work there following the terrorist bombings of 2002. The society that she envisages, and believes in, is dependant on the integrity of each and every individual in it, and not on the effort of or ideology of a single leader. The decision to change and improve society, to effect that transition, must be a self-organised choice for each and every one of us to use our unique positive energy, for the benefit of all humanity.

I am to learn later that this vision and personal philosophy continues to develop with every experience she encounters. It was born, she tells me, like herself, in Yorkshire. A now treasured early memory of Sundays with an unbreakable tradition of dinners with home grown vegetables, roast beef and Yorkshire Pudding, when the whole family would sit down together to eat and to talk. No chattering in these classes for life-long learning, but shrewd guidance and the early setting of standards and challenges. Her dad, back promptly from having a couple of pints in the local pub, at the head of the table inevitably reciting Kipling, 'If you can fill the unforgiving minute with sixty seconds' worth of distance run . . . .' 'We used to look at each other as if to moan and roll our eyes when he was looking the other way,' she says of herself, David, Geoffrey, and Nicola. Now she strews her own conversation with similar quotes, and thanks her good fortune to have had parents who loved literature and learning so much that they both enamoured and carefully endowed all their children with a similar love and respect. 'They turned us out as whole human beings, all beneficially influenced by them she tells me. Fond reminisces bring back the inspiring childhood holiday visits including a favourite to Whitby, learning by heart and keeping it there, the inscription from the monument to the memory of the fearless Captain Cook who sailed from there to Australia.

'To strive, to seek, to find, but not to yield!'

She herself is really inspiring as she speaks of her pride in winning the biggest award in Australia, but evidences her amazement in being chosen for it. These women she is speaking to can't understand that really, because, to a woman, they already instinctively know she is different, deserving and special. They have just seen that month's edition of *Who* listing her, along with Natalie Imbruglia, Jude Law, Crown Prince Frederik of Denmark, Missy Higgins, Kate Winslet, Cate Blanchett, Usher and Mark Webber and the others chosen as the 25 most beautiful

people in the world. Not just people who happen to be beautiful, but truly beautiful people.

She talks about Bali as almost a Damascean revelation, of seeing people working up to eighteen hour days in unison, in a way that she had never experienced before. It was an embracing of race, religion, gender and age that precluded the need for any form of tolerance in a torrent of positive energy. There is a quiet realisation, almost a clouding of collective sadness, so she doesn't have to underline that it takes unthinkable

One of only twenty five, Fiona Wood. *By kind permission of Frances Andrijich*

Dr Fiona Wood and a very happy patient. *The Author*

trauma of this kind to do it. But she insists the trauma is the source of the power that regeneration needs, so even the worst evil can become the oxygen of survival. They are not laughing now, not even smiling, it may be their guilt or contemplative gratitude that they weren't personally involved I am thinking. But I am wrong; at least one of them is a survivor of that holocaust. She quickly alters the mood, and steers them out of that with a deft change of direction.

Back to their day, and she tells them that she is really down from Perth to be there for the Triathlon the next day, and that she has been in daily training for months to be in the 90 km cycle race. In one of these gruelling sessions, she reports being overtaken by a male rider pedalling past her and calling out 'G'day Fiona.' 'It was not the face of the Australian of the Year he recognised,' she laughs, 'it was my ample backside!' They are back on board now, thinking if she might be just like them after all; she wonders if her bum looks big from behind too. She keeps them coming towards her by asking if they have questions. Then it comes, and I'd wager it's the question every woman asks her. How does she cope with all this AND bring up six children?

She tells them that she and Tony didn't plan to have a large family, and points out that they didn't get all six children at once, they just did it. All parents, she reminds them, have to evolve, accommodate and adapt to become a family of three instead of just a couple. The surgeon has them in stitches as she makes light of starting out in the small flat in the London Hospital where they both began their careers, and of leaving stashes of frozen expressed milk about the building when she couldn't have Tom, the first born, with her. 'For years I seemed to be dashing about with a brief case in one hand and a breast pump in the other.' It is transparent that nothing and no-one was ever allowed to stand between the two of them and their growing family. Their priorities are equally clear, the children, their working requirements and then all the other things in life. 'They travel with us still, they are a part of us and we are a part of them. We are a family, so we all have to compromise, but we, as the parents, have to show them how to do that without compromising others.'

Someone asks her if she never feels it's all too much. She nods and grins and recalls one such day when she felt just like that. It had been a tough day at work and on the way home she called at a Supermarket to do a quick food shop. 'The place seemed full of mothers who could enjoy doing the shopping with their children, and for a moment I just couldn't help wishing I was one of them. But there's no time for guilt or self pity once you've made your choices in life, you know,' she tells us. 'You have to be pragmatic. So I left the trolley, drove home, collected all the kids who were in the house at the time, then took them back with me and did the shopping like a full-time mum.'

So when does she find time for herself and how does she relax, someone thinks aloud. She tells them, she loves to start the day with a swim in the ocean, with anyone else who is up early enough or alone if not, and cycling has become a great way of winding down for her. There is no hint of what she had already told me, that on being nominated for the award they sat down as a family and talked through the implications of change for all of them. It had never been unusual for her and Tony to interchange roles in order to support each other's career, Tony changed his practice to accommodate the children. But this was new territory that would affect all their lives, a step that could change the whole family dynamic. Despite this, there was unanimous agreement that she should accept the nomination. On winning she found that the immense increase in work and travel was even greater than anticipated, so she did an audit of her daily routine and time management. At the end of the day she would relax with a glass or two of wine which she said, 'Sometimes left me so relaxed I didn't do anything else! If you accept the honour and privilege of being a public role model, I believe you have to work really hard to justify holding that position.' These were the two hours that she decided she could put to better use.

Looking around the coiffured and manicured room I see many, like me, silently wondering how many of us would have made that particular two hour sacrifice choice. She is extolling the virtues of her 'charmed and occasionally surreal life.' She absolutely believes it, and they can see her glass isn't half full, it's brimming over. Someone asks if the pressure and media attention make for tougher decisions, and does she ever wonder 'Why me?' She responds by identifying the changes that occur for all of us in our lives, emphasising the positive opportunities that we can opt for. 'The toughest decisions for teams like ours are when we have a helpless human being in front of us and know their life is down to us – then we do sometimes wonder.' Then again, with a skill you cannot be trained for, she swings back to the image that they can identify with. 'Another tough decision is what to give six kids to eat that they will all like at the same time!'

That prompts someone to ask what her favourite meal is. 'Anything at all – as long as I haven't had to cook it myself' grins the instantly recognisable mother. They applaud her style, and love her lateral approach to family problem solving as she tells them of an occasion when a couple of the boys made comments about cooking not being one of her strongest points. Swift justice followed as she instantly told them that she was enrolling them both on a cookery course, and did. She does concede however that her victory was rather short-lived, discovering some time later that they had attended as planned, but had switched the cookery lessons for welding. I hear one voice nearby muttering, 'She might not be the best cook in the world but she could definitely take the heat out of my kitchen!'

Another woman expresses the view that she could not handle the pressure of having so much attention focussed on her. Explaining again, that she is always part of a team which helps, and that it was part of her upbringing to see every experience as a new opportunity for learning, and that she does that still, Fiona Wood does concede that there are times when she just has to kick the door and walk away. 'One thing I do know is that I'm a rabid optimist,' she tells them, 'and that is an enormous help in one part of the job that is always hard. 'That is trying to keep the team believing that we are all learning and improving every day. However painful, traumatic or tragic the day has been, and God knows we have had some, what we have learnt today will enable us to do better in helping patients tomorrow.' Just two months later I will be watching bleak, stark and shocking TV newscasts at home, and wishing we had her there to inspire a July bomb-ravaged London.

There is always the risk that the respect and admiration she receives could edge over into adulation, but she won't let that happen. 'We all make the best decision we can at a given time,' she reminds them, 'but that doesn't mean we always make the right one.' She brings them back to earth by recounting how one morning she saw her eldest son, then aged five, spilling a cup of black coffee down the front of his chest and legs. 'Grabbing him in a Half-Nelson, I raced into the shower and held him under the cold jet whilst he screamed to his dad that I was freezing him to death.' Certain she was applying the correct treatment, she held on as Tony appeared calmly asking, 'What are you doing? I haven't put the kettle on yet, that was last night's coffee.' Making one point, she extends it to another, saying how her profession is learning new reactions and approaches in emergency situations now. Booby traps and bombs are teaching them that being a part of the team now means that medics have to wait for a site to be designated as safe before they can rush in to do their work.

With question time over there is a rush of people to meet and have photographs taken with her. She smilingly accommodates all before grabbing me and a chicken leg to eat on the way to our next stop, Bunbury High School – exactly ten minutes behind schedule. I know the routine by now; she races ahead whilst the Headmaster escorts me at a slower pace welcoming me to Australia, the school and this their very special day, because she is there. The Sports Hall that we enter contains about a thousand children, plus staff and other adults.

Fiona is already on stage, microphone in hand addressing the crowd as we arrive and sit at the back of the vast hall, just at the moment that the public address system breaks down. She taps the mike then looks around, as does everyone else, to see who is on hand to fix it. It is very soon clear that no-one can. Two hours earlier I had heard her telling her audience that you just have to keep going when things go wrong. She does. There is no sign of panic, nor impatience or even hesitation. She simply carries on raising her voice to a level we can clearly hear at the back of the hall, and for forty five minutes at stentorian pitch has the undivided attention of everyone in the place. Demonstrating an obvious rapport with children, in an easy style she sets about delivering her message to them at their own level.

She doesn't pull any punches though, first of all telling them how lucky they are, and then asking them what they intend to do with their privilege of education. She's too astute to wait for shrugged shoulders,

Early work in Africa. *The Wood's family collection*

cupped-hand asides or whispered wisecracks. She storms straight in with quick tales of her life to date, full of learning and practising medicine whilst working in Africa, India and on the Chinese Borders, and they wait to hear Bali. She throws in a memorable situation in one country when children were devastated as in one day 700 teachers did not come to school. Smiles that come too early rapidly disappear as she points out that they were not late or temporarily absent, but dead. She doesn't have to make the point, they know it isn't funny now as little waves of realisation appear, that just may be, not being made to learn, but actually wanting to, is special, and being allowed to for some is a real privilege.

She does the 'think you're cool?' bit, and they think it is funny, that she once thought wearing loon pants was cool. Adults in the room share smiles wrapped in beehive hair memories, along with mini skirts, platforms, flares, and shoulders once so wide standing balance was at risk. It's her springboard for celebrating diversity. She expunges the notion of what we call tolerance and replaces it with an all-embracing unconditional acceptance of each by each of us, both collectively and individually. They already know who and what she is, but she decides to give them a taste of a typical day's work describing treating a five year old boy, so badly scalded that he could no longer move his limbs, muscles, nerves or bones. Now as they begin to understand why they are lucky she aims at their potential. She challenges them to unlock their individual skills, to unharness their talents and concentrate on positive action. She throws down the gauntlet of never criticising unless they can offer a better solution. Then she dares them to go on their own fascinating journey of being stretched beyond their expectations. She tells them of Bali but only as an amazing world where human beings, often complete strangers to each other, worked together night and day in total harmony and unison to save the lives of other strangers. They get the message.

I have watched and even taken gatherings in school assemblies for over thirty years and I am waiting throughout for the predictable lull, the drop in interest that is usually heralded by coughs, turning heads and shuffling feet. The sheer size of this place is big enough to do it, but with no microphone it seems almost inevitable. Not with this lady though. She reels them in and lets them out like an expert. The final proof, if needed, comes as she finishes and the time for questions comes. With still no sign of the PA system being back in operation, and an eye on the clock, the children are told that if they do have a question they will have to go down to the front and on to the stage to ask it – without the microphone. It is now predictable that we will pick up our lost ten minutes as the likelihood of teenagers doing that is somewhat remote.

Then there they go, girls, boys, small, tall, curious, shy, cool, articulate, brave and nervous, so many that they have to be stopped. They are oblivious to peer pressure and run a gauntlet walk to the front, climb the stairs and then shake the hand and stand side by side with the Australian of the Year. As some realise where their enthused response has taken them, begetting a full range of treble and half-broken voices from almost inaudible quivering to proudly confident, they ask their questions one by one. Professor Fiona Wood answers each one in general terms but with a cleverly spontaneous customised slant re-enforcing each time how unique, how different, how special they are. They hear the gospel of maximisation of potential, and that being less good than you can be is no good at all, not for you or anyone else. I wait for the loud amen. It is silent, but I can hear it, and there are little flashes of recognition when she offers them the secret of happiness. It is succeeding at what you attempt. She wagers to a grinning response that they have never seen anybody winning and frowning at the same time.

She weaves in the importance of problem solving and facing big challenges head on. When she asks if Maths exams pose a big challenge, half the heads in the place nod. They nod too when they learn that being individual does not absolve them from being active, caring, sharing members of the community with survival strategies alongside probity. As they realise too that by taking responsibility for their own life- style and health they would not only enjoy life more, but incidentally reduce the burden on the national health budget, even their young eyes see the prospect of a better world. The questions keep on coming, from which is the worst burns case she has ever seen, to one little one asking what is the most enjoyable thing about her work. The worst is 'the one I'm seeing today' and the most enjoyable for her 'and for any doctor, is seeing someone who gave you their implicit trust get well again.' They are mixed, some probing, advanced, medically aware and interested in skin, surgery and how she developed the spray technique; some naïve, basic, curious, about her, the people she has met and her own childhood and her children.

She leaves them with a question that she constantly puts to herself and that they could ask themselves, 'How could I do better from what I have learnt today?' She doesn't wait for their considerations, moving straight on to her own strategy; 'Relax, step back from it, identify what happened and get straight back in there.' It moves them one step on from 'What have I done today to make me feel proud?' She reminds them that they each have individual creative power to be effective, like a little pebble thrown into a big pond rippling out benefit for all around them. Then she sets the goal, telling them of the buzz you get when you are stretched further than you thought you could go. Boundaries are there

Children from
Bunbury with the
Australian of the Year.
The Author

to be pushed, and they should push them as far as they can to ensure that they do more than dream of achieving; they will actually achieve. It's Nelson Mandela – Fiona Wood style.

It's a classic condensed course in how to inspire youngsters aged eleven to sixteen. They are boys and girls of all abilities, in an audience of a thousand, and I'm mentally trying to push my own boundaries to think of a way of bottling her, and taking her back with me. Half an hour later after more people, handshakes, photographs, questions, a cup of tea and a piece of chocolate cake, I find that she does have an Achilles heel after all. She can't face singing in public! She has set me up as an unlikely stand-in for her when asked to lead them in singing 'I am Australian.' They are unrehearsed, I have never even heard it sung before, I cannot read music and am stone cold sober, not my usual preferred singing status. But I still venture to think that I cannot be faulted on the grounds of raw enthusiasm. She genuinely seems not to mind that the performance was terrible, bad enough to have us all thrown out at the first audition of *X Factor*. With that bit over, I am seriously relieved that we are dashing back to the car with calls coming in and are on the road heading back to Busselton.

Having been a mere observer all day I am never-the-less grateful to be dropped off to sit and have a chat with Delia's mother, whilst Delia and Fiona do a two hour practice cycling session, following which she picks me up, reloads the bike and drives to our hotel. She suggests I change into something more formal for the evening as we are going to a black tie dinner. I relax and am able to reflect on the day for a full fifteen minutes before she's knocking on the door, showered, dressed and raring to go. I make a mental note to suss out what those energy drinks are and have a shipload sent home.

She's back behind the wheel again and this time we are heading off to meet two hundred GPs from the region, together with their wives, for their Annual Dinner. This one, I note, is different as she switches on the PowerPoint, but it's for their benefit not hers. Still she uses no notes, and there are no hesitations, no repetition, she is in her own field and in even stronger delivery mode now. Sharp, crisp, high-powered, convincing, assured in technical detail, she defines her work 'so far' and outlines her aspirations for the future. 'The challenge for plastic surgeons is to ensure that the scar quality is worth the pain of survival.' So for her scarless healing of wounds is the goal, not the dream. She presents and argues the facts and figures, logic, research, scientific objectivity and empiricism, all combined, with her reactions and observations. From her very early experiences at East Grinstead, when she saw for the first time the results after treatment on world war two victims, she has held the belief, 'We have to be able to do better than this!' They have had a very good dinner and equally good wines but now they are re-focussed and totally absorbed.

It's the power of one, that elixir of leadership she has, and it's strange in combination with her delightfully easy and youthful charisma. She asserts modern technology's power to break down barriers, but adds the

Laboratory work with Dr Marie Stoner. *By kind permission of Frances Andrijich*

caveat that the same power is equally at risk of creating barriers through a division of haves and have-nots. She forecasts radical changes in medicine that will impact on the fibre of society, with doctors being less of a scientific, technical driving force, to become leaders of a progressive debate for a framework of social inclusion. She tells them more, deeper and differently, than she had told the other audiences. Medical statistics are clinically reported, ' . . . 28 patients suffering from between 2% and 92% body burns, deadly infections and delayed shock, emotional trauma . . . .' Every action taken in those terrible days after the atrocity had additionally to become research. 'We had to make sure that every patient we treated was a step forward in the evolution of clinical care, so we didn't lose a single lesson,' says the member of the team which had to be directed to take time to rest from attending to the needs of the victims. She again invites the challenging of assumptions such as 'burns will always scar,' clarifying her intention that it will not always be so. It's part of the vision again, the roles that can be played with the amazing variety of skills available.

They know what I didn't know, that this team had the foresight to plan a response to a major disaster five years before Bali 2002 called it into action. They knew also of the quality of her work with scientist Dr. Marie Stoner in founding the McComb Foundation in 1999, their long-term research and their subsequent, revolutionary results in reducing healing time through Clinical Cell Culture. Her world leading and ground-breaking use of tissue engineering technology is held in the highest regard in their specialist world, where they have observed the results of patients' own culture- grown skin sprayed back on to the burns area. Instead of the traditional 21 days it would have taken to produce the requisite cells following a skin graft, it could now be reduced to as little as 5 days. The implications, not just medically, but financially too, become clear now, even to me. The Foundation's self-funding research continues with the vision of no child growing up bearing physical scars inching nearer and nearer. It is not a political slogan or a noble gesture. It is quite simply what she intends to achieve.

What they don't hear, because it might seem to be boasting, is that of all the innumerable visitors to the Burns Unit, one visit, the previous month, had particular significance for her. Not simply because he had taken the trouble to 'do his homework' before the visit, or because he clearly had a genuine interest and an informed view of the work already achieved, not even because he was from the old country and is its future king. His Royal Highness The Prince of Wales over-ran on his schedule by almost an hour as he chatted to patients and questioned Fiona Wood and the team. 'His visit was so important to all of us because it was so plain he wasn't just making an effort, he was very supportive. It wasn't

HRH The Prince of Wales' visit to the Royal Perth Hospital. *Fiona Wood's collection*

meant to be a public visit, a media event; it really was for him to learn more about the work he already had an awareness of.'

Her vision absorbs all it implies, but is strengthened by what she has witnessed. Unsensationally she talks these colleagues through her patients' cycles of pain, long-term immobilisation, dressings, more pain, physiotherapy, more pain, treatment, more pain, surgery and yet more pain. The intensity of their pain sears through her account, as she describes the team's efforts to minimize it, and reminds us that it can be difficult to observe, just as it is to endure. Always with the plight and needs of the patients at the fore, she adds the violent colour of the impact on staff to the scenes. If then, after all the work and the caring and the sharing, they have to face the reality of the patient dying, they are as if a part of the bereaved family. Then, of her own reactions she says, 'You'd be a hard man not to have a few tears. The only place to go is where you can just have a good cry, because then you have to go back to the team and convince them that they did a good job. Then you all cry together!' These teams worked the long hours of disaster planning and had to be ordered to leave their posts in the constant rebuilding of faces and bodies and lives, to sleep for a few hours or eat. She knows the exact hour and date that three of her patients died in those dreadful days; one on the third day, one on the sixth and one on the twentieth.

That this audience understands and shares more of this than I have the capacity to do is evidenced in the quality and depth of their questioning. They are testing, learning, probing almost, urging her to go on so they can know more too, and maybe even feel a greater part of it all. It has the feel of being one of those never to be forgotten frissons, a 'where were you when?' moment. I sense it is a part of her personal survival strategy, that the horror of Bali was an ill wind that could yet have brought some good through its legacy to research, treatment healing and practice.

You know that despite those 18 and 20 hour days, she knows each and every single one of those human beings. She knows by heart, their names as well as their case histories, whether they have families, what their other dreams are, but also instinctively whether they are strong or they will need massive aftercare. Some of them are able to accept that there is an opportunity in, or even because of the hell they are in, to re-shape and re-define who they are. So many of them, she is fiercely proud to report, do make massive adjustments and answer their own questions as to what has become important in life. You start to know why they not only respect but love her so much in both her modes. The seemingly indefatigable and tireless expert, a masked and gowned surgeon or the chic, bespoke dressed and customised jewellery wearing young woman, chatting and laughing her way round ward and clinic. She is a Broome pearled, walking talking contradiction in terms, female force wrapped in feminine frivolity. It's why amongst scores of other awards she has been voted A Living National Treasure and for the second year running The Most Trusted Person in Australia.

She can't heal invisible scars though, her own and the pain of sharing others' pain is with her still, and it's tangible at moments like this. I realise that I have never really grasped the depth and extent of anguish in such commitment and involvement for the medical practitioner in these terms. My own limited, though grateful perspective, has been as the patient, the bereaved family or as a friend. I think it was at this point that I began to see that I was observing someone far beyond my understanding. But she herself doesn't understand all of it, and certainly not the respect that people have for her. We leave the dining room, applause still ringing behind us and people standing up to shake her hand, not unlike the children earlier in the day, it occurs to me, but not to her. Her last remark to the woman who follows her to the door thanking her is that she hopes that tomorrow she will not finish as badly as she did the previous year in the cycle race. She really doesn't grasp it. In their eyes, she could not do badly in anything and she has no weaknesses. I suddenly have an overwhelming wish that her mother and father were here and had spent this remarkable day with us.

I am enthused to the point of inspiration by her, but a mere observer of her day, am also physically and emotionally drained. Never-the-less I venture one last question for her. Has today been a typical day in the life of Fiona Wood? In the headlights of oncoming traffic I see the grin change her profile and hear 'No, of course not. Days like this are special for me, I really enjoy them.' Then the grin fades to nothing as she adds 'I've had no clinics or surgery to do today. Surgically removing burnt flesh off human bodies, that's a hard day's work, Mel.' I am silent for the remainder of the journey back to the hotel. After telling me we will meet up at seven the next morning, and explaining who will be where and doing what the next day, she dashes off to catch up with Tony and four of the children who have arrived in our absence. And I crawl into bed.

It's another sunshine day in Busselton and I am on the beach by seven thirty, after being collected from the hotel by Jenni Ballantyne and her husband Kurt. They are friends of the Kieraths I learn, Kurt competing in the half marathon in another team in the triathlon. Jenni is generally helping out and supporting everyone including Fiona on the bike for 90 kilometres, Tony doing the 6 kilometre swim, and their eldest son, Tom, running the 20 kilometre leg. I am

on sunscreen and water distribution, taking photos and cheering louder than the three remaining, younger children.

I am also first into the First Aid tent, with a bite on my shin as big and ugly as a clenched fist. It is frighteningly purple, but I am stoic and unconcerned, secure in the knowledge that I shall soon be sorted out by the best First Aiders in the world. I remind myself that they have expertise of a calibre that had been sound enough to beat Grimethorpe in the Commonwealth Junior Cadet St John's Ambulance Brigade Championships in Perth only two months earlier. World rating was Australia first, New Zealand second, and

Tom Wood – one third of the Iron Man triathlon. *The Author*

The Grimethorpe St John's Ambulance Cadet Team – Instructor Terry Haye MBE, Matthew Lomas, Katy Lomas, Karina and Kirsty Johnson and Adam Kemp with the Mayor and Mayoress of Barnsley greeted by the Mayor of Perth. Matthew Lomas was 1st out of 360 in the individual cadets class. *The Mayor's collection.*

Grimethorpe third. These attendants are not the juniors, they are the real McCoy. As I leave the tent seconds later, holding the tiny plaster I have been given to stick over the monstrous thing, which is now the size of a hamster clinging to my shin, I silently wonder if the way that water goes down a plughole might have had anything to do with the outcome of that contest. After all, questions on how to remove venom from a snake bite or what to do if bitten by a redback spider don't crop up that often in Grimethorpe.

And anyway, I can remember as a child, having had a bigger plaster than this put on for me, and on a smaller graze on a much smaller leg, in the Ambulance Room at Grimethorpe Colliery, after falling off the bus step one Friday when I went with my dad to collect his wage. I feel an overwhelming urge to limp back in and tell them that, but I'm conscious of the need not to be rated a sore loser or a whingeing Pom, so I hobble bravely back across the field to take a seat in a distant deck chair. I miss Fiona streaking past on the bike as I continue to examine more closely the now throbbing limb and try to whinge silently. I am also trying to work out what colour a cardinal-purple leg with freckles would have to go before it would require a second application of factor 35 sunscreen under an antipodean sun beating down on it.

The day is otherwise wonderful, healthily competitive and Fiona, Tony and Tom all finish, happy with improvements on their previous personal best and with Delia's team winning the women's open division. I have a choice to make, to stay for the barbecue and go back to Perth the next day with Fiona – at 5am; or to go back that evening with Jenni and Kurt. The next morning the bite is now too swollen to lift without the help of a crane, so I opt for the second option. It turns out to be a good move as I am able to hear more of the achievements (that Fiona would never tell me about herself, of course.) On my travels from Los Angeles to Fiji to Perth, I had found a universal respect and gratitude, and an almost iconic admiration for Fiona Wood. Everywhere her name was mentioned – from ever smiling Bula Bula Fijians to never smiling G'day Bruces there was genuine warmth in the response to it. These close friends attempted to share an objective judgement, but confirmed all I had heard about her, and more. They were curious to hear how I had heard of her achievements when it seemed that there had been no real acknowledgement of her work in England. Beyond the reach of BBC *Look North* and YTV *Calendar*, the *Yorkshire Post* and *Barnsley Chronicle* at that point it was true. But the mills of God are grinding now. Barnsley Metropolitan Borough Council held the first civic reception in the UK for her, presenting a letter from Prince Charles commending her work. The Yorkshire Society has made her an

Elsie Wood, Jess Keirath, Fiona Wood, Geoff Wood and Nicola Halafihi arriving at Barnsley Town Hall for the first civic recognition in the UK of Dr Wood's achievements. *The Author*

The Wood family greeted by the Mayor and Mayoress of Barnsley, Cllr. Joe Hayward and Pauline Haigh, and the Deputy Mayor and Mayoress Cllr Roy and Christine Miller. *The Author*

Honorary Vice President, and in July 2007she is has an honorary degree from the University of Leeds.

As we drove north, Jenni commented on the similarity of my accent to Fiona's and also likened it to that of the Calendar Girls. 'I met some of them once,' she told me, instantly closing the world to the size of the A59. 'I sat next to them on an aircraft flying to England after they had been to the premiere of the film over here.' You couldn't put odds on that could you? I had been on the biggest island in the world for three days and had bumped into the only other person I had actually heard of before I came; the woman who had sparked off my trip off in the first place. I couldn't wait to tell Ros Fawcett.

An early morning call from the other woman I had come to know invites me to share Mothers' Day with her and some of her children. There is no sentimentality about who is there for the day. Evie, the youngest, and Jack are still with the family of friends they were travelling back from Busselton with. Jess is in residence near the hospital where she studies, medicine of course, and Tom and Tony are still not back from Busselton either, possibly still recovering from the triathlon. So we settle for a lunch on the beach with Joe and Dan. I have learnt so

Jenni Ballantyne and
Tony Keirath.
The Author

much from her over this weekend including, for the first time, what freedom and boundlessly unrestricted variety of choice of contact within a bigger family is like, and find it a strange contrast to having always spent the day with my 'only two' children.

Having met all six children I now realise that the question is not how does she cope with six children as well as everything else she does? It is how does any couple get six such great kids? She says they have their moments but I am seeing stable, happy, easy-going, caring, sharing, personable, bright and beautiful young individuals, whose advantage in terms of likely success is in another world from that of their grandparents, and yet look at what they achieved.

So when I finally leave them, the last questions are for myself. If these youngsters represent the kind of development we would wish for every child, how can we do it? Just what is that indefinable quality that schools are now expected to teach as a subject, a real X Factor; and how can we, who do not possess it ourselves, manage that? Will systems which have already failed be 're-discovered', funded as initiatives and spun as progress? How and by whom, will decisions which wipe out 'obsolete' areas of learning like home-making, cookery, craft and now the arts, be made? Have 'they' yet learnt not to throw the baby out with the bath water? Does raising the school leaving age actually improve the quality of education or merely extend the time allowed for its completion? How many teachers today actually enjoy their work? Should we stop giving awards and Ofsted ratings for outstanding teacher performance and substitute better systems for them and others to teach without disruption? What are we testing for? How and what do tests currently contribute in terms of diagnostic teaching and learning development? Are systems flexible enough to maximise the potential of late developers? Fiona Wood tells me that before she became Head Girl at Ackworth School she had failed her 11-Plus. 'I was just another failure at that stage,' she tells me. It was only her parents' insistence that she had both ability and the character to use it, which restored her confidence and motivated her.

It is what every person who teaches, whether formally trained to do so or not, instinctively knows. With the right family care, love, support, faith and encouragement virtually any learning disadvantage can be overcome. Compensation, for where that is not available, will still have to come from hardworking, committed professionals with leadership to match. Their vision, instinct and effort will remain, to work through whatever it takes to support and develop the potential of every child. Despite the imposition of further policy changes and legislation, they will circle the system again and again, whilst someone designs expensive new clothes for the Emperor; or after consultation and extensive research the wheel is re-invented.

I wonder about some of those policies, deemed 'passé' but so firmly founded in the work of the real teachers; great educators in practice, led by the likes of the Sadlers, Cleggs and Attenboroughs, to ensure access to appropriate skills through education suited to ability and aptitude. What it takes to make the difference between having the dream, or living it, hangs in the balance, and initiative is easily buried under paper. I think back to my lovely long chats, reminiscing with Fiona Wood's mother and father and the times we felt we were 'not able to'. They are symptomatic of that rare breed; people who won't accept 'not able' so deftly changed the label. They became and produced new generations of learners and teachers whose contributions are notable. They lived through times when medicine, teaching and the like were respected and accepted as noble professions. Fiona Wood would cringe at the word but she is; and more than noble, she is the stuff Nobels are made of.

But what is it that drives her? The scientist responds with another quote from the arts:

'Life is no brief candle to me, it is a flaming torch that I have got hold of for a moment and I want to make it burn as brightly as possible before handing it on to future generations.'

Final Acknowledgements

The following people have made contributions in a number of ways for which I thank them all. Their creative ideas, constructive criticism, professional advice, physical support, mechanical assistance, photographs, paintings, encouragement and hospitality have enabled me to complete a lengthy and sometimes demanding, but mostly enjoyable and fascinating task:

Christa Ackroyd
Susan Andrew
Gaynor Barnes
Dickie Bird
John Bostick
Dermot Bradley
Martin Brook
Derek Carpenter
Christine Clancy
Dean Cook
Jean Cryne
Shaun Dooley
Alex Durasow
Keith Ellis
Marilyn Esquivel
Roy Fellowes
Leanne Goacher
Vic Grainger
Pauline Haigh
Joanne Harris
Louise Hewitt
Jane Hickson
Trevor Holroyd
Margaret Hunter
Kathy Jackson
Anne Kelly
Katy Kennedy
Paul Lafferty
Sybil Maley
Lord Mason
Cllr Roy Miller

Fernando Alvarez
Nick Auckland
Suzanne Bell
Jessica Booth
Rachael Boycott
Hazel Broadhead
Phil Butler
Val Carpenter
Lady Clegg
Jay Cooper
Debbie Dolan
John Dossett
John Edwards
Eileen Ellis
Chris Evans
Bill Fisher
Diana Gilfillan
Daniel Greenfield-Turton
Sir Ernest Hall
Jacob Hawkins
Ian Hey
Ella Hinchliffe
Cllr Steve Houghton
Lisa Hutton
Daniel Jenkinson
Steve Kempe
Andy Kershaw
Michael Lindley
David Markwell
Ian McKinlay
Cllr Margaret Morgan

Helen Anderson
Nick Balac
Rodney Bickerstaffe
Mark Booth
Geoffrey Boycott
Jason Brook
Ken Capstick
Pamela Caunt
James Cole
Phil Coppard
Beth Dolan
Jayne Dowle
Murray Edwards
Tim Elmhirst
Roz Fawcett
David Frances
Colin Goulding
George Gregg
Muriel Hampshire
Cllr Joe Hayward
Sue Hey
Carolyn Hodgson
Steve Huison
Ashley Jackson
Tom Jewkes
Joshua Kennedy
Melanie Killilea
Keith Madeley
Billy Marsden
Christine Miller
Josie Muxlowe

Terry Mullen
Graham Myers
Richard Northern
Alex Rennick
Polly Rennison
Peter Rowbotham
Kevin Sharp
Shaun Smith
Debbie Somers
Cassandra Sweet
Phil Thompson
Daryl Topliss
Billy Turton
Cyndi Wakita
John Warburton
Rev Ian Wildey
Geoff Wood

Alex Myers
Cllr Bill Newman
Ben Platts
Donna Rennison
Steve Rennison
Kathy Savile
Sue Sharp
Theresa Smith
Katherine Sunderland
Christine Talbot
Ned Thacker
David Topliss
Jake Utley
Dick Walker
Sam Wichelow
Kathleen Wilkinson

David Myers
Cllr Pat Newman
Connor Ramskill
Olivia Rennison
Katherine Richardson
Chris Sedgewick
Christina Shaw
David Sugden
Mike Swallow
Joanne Tasker
Len Tingle
William Turner
Lydia Utley
Graham Walker
Liz Wildey
Elsie Wood